Scottish Highland
RAILWAYS

West Highland Line between Tyndrum and Bridge of Orchy, looking to Beinn Odhar.

Scottish Highland
RAILWAYS

DAVID TUCKER

THE CROWOOD PRESS

First published in 2021 by
The Crowood Press Ltd
Ramsbury, Marlborough
Wiltshire SN8 2HR

enquiries@crowood.com

www.crowood.com

British Library Cataloguing-in-Publication Data
A catalogue record for this book is available from the British Library.

ISBN 978 1 78500 792 7

Illustrations
The majority of the photographs are the author's originals; others are credited individually. With special acknowledgment to the following: the Museum of Scottish Railways (The Scottish Railway Preservation Society), John Robin, Norman McNab, Sarah Bromage, iStock.com by Getty Images (various individuals), Picfair (various individuals), Wikimedia Commons and Open Street Map.

Typeset by Jean Cussons Typsetting, Diss, Norfolk

Printed and bound in India by Replika Press Pvt Ltd

Contents

Preface, Definitions and Terminology

Scottish Highland Railways is one of a series of railway books from Crowood that cover both the hobby of modelling (more than fifty titles published) and the history of the railways themselves. Since 2014 the latter titles have covered, on a regional basis, the railways of Lincolnshire, Shropshire, Ayrshire, Telford and other UK regions.

The present book differs from these published titles in a crucial way, due to the vast geographical scale of railways serving the Highlands of Scotland. There are eight long lines running into and through the Highlands, plus, of course, the 'lost lines' that any regional history must cover. This scale reduces the opportunity for providing too much local detail, although the book does include extensive sourcing and referencing for those wishing to delve into local, historical railway detail (for example, books focusing on the West Highland Line or the Great North of Scotland company, and also online resources). There is no shortage of publications and online sources covering the history of the railways in Scotland, among them P.J.G. Ransom's comprehensive *Iron Road – The Railway in Scotland* (Berlinn, 2007), David Spaven's *The Railway Atlas of Scotland* (also from Berlinn, 2015) and *Getting the Train: The History of Scotland's Railways*, by David Ross (Stenlake, 2018).

The geographical extent and the nature of the network in the Highlands means that history is best dealt with line by line, rather than in a strict chronology of railway companies. There was originally little in common between, for example, the Duke's railway in distant Sutherland and the West Highland connecting Helensburgh to Glasgow, or the Royal Deeside line taking Queen Victoria and her guests to Balmoral Castle. A strict chronological approach would drag the reader from one side of Scotland to the other within each of the formative decades (for example, the 1890s) so chronology is presented within the chapters dedicated to each of the distinct railway lines (for example West Highland, East Coast, Far North).

An exception can be made, however, for the single chapter covering the twentieth century. It may seem odd to offer several chapters covering line development between 1840 and 1900 and only one for the twentieth century, but as the introduction to that chapter will explain, the Highland railway network was more or less complete by the early 1890s, and the main changes affecting it in the twentieth century would be national – or even international – rather than localized. These included the impact of two World Wars, the 'Grouping' into larger rail companies, nationalization (into British Railways) and then privatization, these events accompanied by broad social and technological changes: the rise of car ownership, the demise of steam, and the impact of 'Beeching' (explained below under Terminology).

Although historical by nature, the book also examines trends and events in the early twenty-first century that are underpinned not only by changes in railway management (the franchise system), but also by technology and political changes, such as devolved powers for the Scottish government regarding public transport. This century has also brought a refreshing revival of interest in both modern rail and heritage lines, not least among tourists to Scotland interested in riding *The Jacobite* steam-hauled trains over the Glenfinnan viaduct, made world famous in the Harry Potter movies.

Note on publication date: This book was written mainly during 2019 for publication in early 2020 but the global pandemic caused by the COVID-19 virus delayed publication into 2021. The pandemic and its 'lockdown' also delayed impending government decisions on the future of UK railways (the postponed Williams Review) and, in Scotland, on the ScotRail franchise. Furthermore, the pandemic introduced uncertainty over the UK's planned exit from the European Union ('Brexit') that would ultimately influence railways in the Scottish Highlands.

Given its historical emphasis, the book was not greatly affected by the events of 2020, but the perspective of Chapter 9, *Scottish Highland Railways in the Twenty-First Century*, should be read in this context.

Defining the Highlands

There is a geological definition enshrined in the Highland Boundary Fault, but this has little relevance in terms of human settlement and therefore of the transport network. Instead, coverage starts at the northern extremity of the Central Belt – the low-lying area stretching from Glasgow to Edinburgh – and extends all the way northwards to the coast at the UK's most northerly railway station, Thurso, by way of Fort William in the west, Inverness in the centre and Aberdeen in the east.

MODERN GOVERNMENT AREAS (COUNCILS) IN THE HIGHLANDS

COUNCIL AREA	PRINCIPAL SETTLEMENTS*
Highland Council	Inverness, Nairn, Fort William, Thurso, Wick, Dingwall
City of Aberdeen	–
Aberdeenshire	Peterhead,* Fraserburgh,* Inverurie, Stonehaven
Moray	Elgin, Forres, Buckie/Rathven*
Perth and Kinross (north)	Perth, Crieff,* Dunkeld, Pitlochry
Argyll and Bute (north)	Oban
Stirling (north and west)	Stirling, Callander*
Angus (north)	Dundee, Arbroath, Forfar,* Montrose, Carnoustie

* not served by rail in 2019

Politically, Highland Council is the largest of the local government areas in Britain, with an area of nearly 10,000 square miles (including the former counties or shires of Inverness, Ross, Cromarty, Caithness and Sutherland). The term 'Highlands and Islands' is still used by some organizations (for example by HITRANS – Highlands and Islands Transport Partnership), but it now has no political relevance. The islands – the Hebrides, Orkney and Shetland – have no railways, but there are important links from ports with railway stations for transferring to ferries (Aberdeen, Oban, Mallaig, Kyle of Lochalsh, Thurso and Wick).

Like 'Highlands and Islands', 'Grampian' has disappeared from the political lexicon but remains useful for defining a large north-eastern corner of Scotland, nowadays containing the council areas of Aberdeen City, Aberdeenshire and Moray. An understanding of railway development in this region is crucial to understanding the evolution of northern Scottish railways.

Finally, there are Highland lines that start (or end) in the northern reaches of the counties of Perth and Kinross, Argyll and Bute, Stirling and Angus, and all these therefore straddle 'highland' and 'lowland' and need to be considered.

Terminology

With the general reader in mind, technical terms (and abbreviations) are avoided as much as possible, but there needs to be some clarification of basic terms involving the railway system, traction, and the companies responsible for the network's development in the Scottish Highlands.

Please note that ScotRail's website is scotrail.co.uk. There is an unofficial website called scot-rail.co.uk for 'Scotland's online rail enthusiast community', while Railscot (railscot.co.uk) is an unofficial, primary resource for Scottish railway information.

Railway Terms

'Rail' is used interchangeably with 'railway' to describe both the industry as a whole and the companies involved, while a railway is also the actual 'permanent way' comprising trackbed, track, sleepers. Routes are described as 'lines' between two termini, both informally and to denote specific ScotRail terms: Kyle Line, Far North Line *et al.*

'Train' should not be used to denote a locomotive, which is the vehicle that provides the traction, whether steam, diesel or electric. Where used, 'train' refers to a group of connected railway carriages or wagons hauled by a locomotive engine (described together as the rolling stock), and usually specific to a route and service (for example, the 9.10 train from Helensburgh to Fort William). A train may include multiple units, where an engine is incorporated into at least one of the carriages to make them self-propelled (either diesel or electric, DMU or EMU).

Companies

The main government franchise for passenger services in Scotland is branded as ScotRail, the franchise held since 2015 by Abellio, based in the Netherlands (hence, 'Abellio ScotRail Ltd'). Other companies with passenger services reaching the Highlands are LNER ('London North Eastern Railway'), Caledonian Sleeper (operated by Serco) and Cross-Country (by Arriva). Freight services, which are not covered in this book, are contracted by separate companies.

Early rail companies in the Highlands often had long, complicated names – an exception being Highland Railway, founded and named in 1865, an early company whose role should not be confused with the overall railway structure of the Highlands, as defined in Chapter 1. In this book, three conventions are used to shorten and simplify these long names: any 'The' prefix, and the suffixes 'Railway' and 'Junction', are omitted, and an ampersand (&) is used for the many companies whose names usually bore their destinations – for example Dunblane, Doune & Callander (rather than 'The Dunblane, Doune and Callander Railway'); Scottish Central; or Keith & Dufftown.

Abbreviations for companies are prolific in the rail industry but are avoided where possible in this book. The essential ones are these:

- BR: British Rail. From 1946 to 1994, railways in Scotland were operated under the nationalized BR system as its Scottish Region
- The 'big four' private groups that preceded BR were LMS (London Midland & Scottish), LNER (London & North Eastern), Great Western Railway (GWR) and Southern Railway (SR), of which only LMS and LNER operated in Scotland. (The LNER name was revived in 2018 as the name of the new franchise holder for the East Coast line – London to Scotland – replacing Virgin)
- Preceding LMS and LNER in the Highlands were, principally, Highland Railway and Great North of Scotland (GNOS)

On a carriage, the official colour scheme and script for ScotRail including a Gaelic translation.

Traction and Rolling Stock

The electrification of lines is taking place in Central Scotland with the goal of reducing the use of diesel engines. The most common traction in the Highlands, however, is still provided by DMU. In 2019, Abellio ScotRail's locomotive fleet numbered just over 500, with an increasing proportion of EMU.

In the Highlands, high speed trains (HST) have been hauled, until 2019, by Class 43 (or 'InterCity 125') diesel on the long-distance routes between Glasgow or Edinburgh and Aberdeen or Inverness. From December 2019, LNER planned to use new 'Azuma' (Class 800) sets on the Scottish legs of its long-distance services from London. Class 170 ('Turbostar') still operated in 2019 (for example Aberdeen–Inverness), some cascaded from central Scotland routes, replacing Class 156 ('Super Sprinter', on the West Highland Line) or Class 158 ('Express Sprinter', Far North and Kyle lines). During 2019 and 2020, a number of Class 153 'Super Sprinter' rail-cars were being phased in for the West Highland, Far North and Kyle lines; they couple to other multiple units including Classes 156, 158 and 170. Some carriages using Class 153 on the West Highland were being converted, in 2019, to carry up to twenty bicycles and with more rack space for sports equipment and luggage such as rucksacks.

'Beeching'

Familiar to anyone with an interest in British railway history is the symbolic abbreviation 'Beeching' for the rationalization of the nationalized rail network in the 1960s to 1970s. 'Beeching cuts', or even 'the Beeching axe', are short-hand terms for the large swathe of British railways – encompassing stations and whole lines: a dozen of them within the Highlands – that were closed down. This action followed recommendations in an official repor (*The Reshaping of British Railways*, 1963) written by Dr Richard Beeching, Chairman of British Railways.

Distances

The imperial system is used throughout, in line with UK road distances (still officially measured in miles, not kilometres):

1 mile = 1.6 kilometres
1 yard = 0.9 metres
1 foot (eg 3,000ft) = 30 centimetres. Three feet = 1 yard
1 inch (eg 10in) = 2.54 centimetres. Twelve inches = 1 foot

CHAPTER I

Background to Scotland and its Highland Railways

Railways into and through the Scottish Highlands were shaped by a combination of factors – geographical, political, social and economic – and these factors continue to influence the industry today.

Highland Geography

Beginning with physical geography, the Highlands area (as defined above 'Defining the Highlands') covers 33,300 square miles, or one-third of the land mass of Great Britain. The obvious characteristic of this region is its mountainous or hilly terrain, which has contributed to the sparse population: around six persons per square mile, as against forty per square mile for Scotland as a whole (and 264 per square mile in England). Settlements are widely spread out: some stretches of the journeys through the Highlands involve gaps of more than 15 miles between stations. At one extreme, the last stage on the northbound Main Line between Carrbridge and

View from Duirinish station (single platform), remote request stop on Kyle Line; fewer than 1,000 annual 'entries and exits' are made by passengers at this station (see Appendix 4).

Corrour summit (West Highland Line) in winter. JOHN ROBIN, 1974

Inverness is 27.6 miles, typically lasting 28 minutes, and there are several non-stop runs of 15 miles or more on the rural lines if no 'request stops' are made.

Physical features presented challenges to railway builders in the nineteenth century. The flat east coast route was the easiest, and first, to be developed – *see* Chapter 2 – in part due to a relatively high population density and to thriving agriculture and industry (fishing, forestry), but also inspired by royal approval: Queen Victoria and Prince Albert both approved of train travel, particularly when a line opened to their Highland retreat, Balmoral.

In the centre and west of northern Scotland, tougher terrain meant fewer towns and villages to connect, and the need to build railways around, or over, a variety of physical features. As encountered on each of the lines described in subsequent chapters, these features included mountains and hills (or 'bens', from the Gaelic name, still used); rivers and lakes, or 'lochs'; and valleys both steep ('glens') and broad ('straths'). The route from the southern urban centres (Glasgow, Edinburgh, Perth, Stirling) to Inverness, the Highland capital, was blocked by the Drumochter and Slochd mountain passes until the 1890s, while the fjord-like structure of the indented west coast also delayed the development of a West Highland line.

Climate is another factor for railways to contend with in the Highlands, particularly high winds and snow on the lines in winter.

Highland History

The Highlands took part in Scottish national history, but also had their own historical development, based on early tribal regions and, later, the importance of local extended families known as 'clans'. In the course of describing the development of specific railway lines – and stations, in particular – reference is made to some key events in Scottish history, and these are outlined briefly, as follows:

- Early peoples – Picts, Britons and Scotti, or Scots – left their imprint on the land, particularly in enduring place names (bens, glens) and some monuments. Roman occupation was brief, from *c.* AD70 to *c.* AD212
- Scottish nationhood was confirmed in the medieval period by resistance to attacks from both the English and the Norse. The Stuart dynasty (1371–1714) included kings and queens of both Scotland and, after 1603, England (as the united

Great Britain under James I, but remaining as James VI in Scotland). Ousted by the Hanoverian dynasty, the Stuarts in exile plotted – unsuccessfully – to retake the British throne (*see* sidebar: The Jacobites)

- The eighteenth century brought enlightenment and the Agricultural Revolution, together with the growth of the British Empire, producing an exodus of people from the Highlands. Migration continued into the nineteenth century, when thousands of Highlanders were displaced by sheep farms (during the Clearances); but coastal fishing developed, and Queen Victoria's love of Scotland and its people kick-started tourism to the Scottish Highlands
- The World Wars of the twentieth century united the British in common cause, but by the 1990s the demand for semi-independence ('devolution' of power from Westminster) had reinstated a parliament in Edinburgh with an influence on transport development in Scotland. The old industries declined, but forestry, energy production, leisure and tourism took their place in the Highland economy

The twenty-first century has brought unresolved challenges that warrant their own chapter, including the management of the country's railway system, and, at a higher level, Scotland's position within the United Kingdom (and within Europe).

Highland Culture, Tourism and Railway Journeys

The motivations of rail passengers today are usually very different from those of early nineteenth-century travellers by rail.

Tourists are drawn not only to the Highlands, but also to enjoying its railway journeys: the West Highland Line is regularly voted among the world's most scenic journeys. The tourist is also likely to hope to encounter some aspects of the regional landscape or culture that are very distinctly 'Highland' – almost bordering on cliché!

The cultural symbols of the Highlands, however clichéd, range from tartan and bagpipes to 'hairy cows' and heather, but some of the symbols helped underpin railway development in the tourist era. The chiefs of the clans who dominated some regions often had the final say on railway routes, as the wealthy landowners, and the castles they occupied, were sometimes given private stations (for example Dunrobin in Sutherland, Blair Atholl in Perthshire, Duncraig in Ross-shire). Whisky distilleries were

Queen Victoria's Royal Route, celebrated at the former Ballater station tearoom (described in Chapter 2).

THE JACOBITES

A Jacobite was a supporter of the armed rebellions aimed at restoring the Stuart dynasty to the British throne, starting with the exiled James II of Britain (James VII in Scotland). The King Jameses had styled themselves 'Jacobus', from the Latin, hence 'Jacobite'.

The most serious of several Jacobite risings was the final one, in 1745–46, when Stuart supporters under the exiled Charles Edward Stuart ('Bonnie Prince Charlie') invaded from France, raised armed insurgence in the Highlands and marched south, capturing Edinburgh and driving on to the English Midlands. Forced to retreat by the British army, the last Jacobites were defeated at the Battle of Culloden (1746) near Inverness. The Bonnie Prince escaped to the Hebridean islands and then to France.

The Highland Main Line crosses the Culloden battlefield where the National Trust visitor centre is an important destination for visitors to the Highlands. The West Highland branch to Mallaig stops at Glenfinnan, where Charles gathered his supporters.

The viaduct at Glenfinnan, and *The Jacobite* steam train that crosses it, have since been made famous by Harry Potter movies, and interest in the Jacobites has been fostered by Outlander, a popular series of books and television dramas.

often positioned deliberately off the beaten track – to evade discovery by the excise collector – but transporting raw materials and casks became an important function for rail in some areas.

In the modern era, railways have developed alongside tourism in several directions. ScotRail, the main national operator, offers several tourist 'passes' over several days, including the Highland Rover, Spirit of Scotland and Scottish Grand Tour. Tour companies such as Great Rail Journeys, although based in York, had nineteen tours on sale in 2019, the majority with names such as 'Highland Adventure' and 'Christmas in the Highlands'. Heritage trips are popular, the most familiar being rides on *The Jacobite* (with its Harry Potter connections) by West Coast Railways and the Strathspey Railway, based in the busy tourist town of Aviemore on the Highland main line.

Another distinct cultural feature of travelling in the Highlands comes from encountering the old language of Gaelic. Although spoken today by only a small minority, the language retains its links with the landscape – lochs, bens, glens – and also with towns and their railway stations. Since 1996, ScotRail has put Gaelic translations on station signs, some examples being the following:

Ardlui = Àird Laoigh, meaning 'high ground of the young deer'

Inverness = Inbhir Ness, 'mouth of the River Ness'
Pitlochry = Baile Chloichridh, 'place of the sentinel stone'
Tyndrum Lower = Taigh an Droma Ìochdrach, 'the house on the ridge'

Example of the translated station name at Ardlui (West Highland Line), in English and Gaelic.

The translation of ScotRail itself as Réile na h-Alba – with 'Réile' meaning railway and 'Alba' being the ancient name for Scotland – has been introduced into the livery, along with a saltire symbol.

Infrastructure: Past to Present

The Highland infrastructure for both rail and road transport has been influenced by the geography of this UK region, both physical and human. A mountainous, often rugged terrain means that human settlements – and railway stations – are small and scattered far apart.

Railway lines have to negotiate steep inclines and summits, and must be carved through mountain passes or along river valleys and, frequently, alongside bodies of water: rivers, lakes or the seacoast. These challenges to constructing a railway through semi-wilderness have resulted in scenic enjoyment for passengers, making the journeys more popular among twenty-first-century tourists than ever before.

Highland railway lines are, for the most part, single track, for the obvious reason that traffic is too infrequent to justify double tracking. However, this is changing on the Aberdeen–Inverness line, 108 miles long in total, on which 16 miles of track out of Aberdeen were doubled in 2018/19. (Also on this line, three new stations have been built and platforms lengthened at some stations.)

Single track, doubling temporarily, to loop round the island platform at Ardlui station (West Highland).

The predominant use of single tracking meant that loops for trains to pass, and also sidings, were important elements from the beginning. Island platforms, with up and down trains passing on each side, are frequently found on Highland lines, usually necessitating tunnelled walkways for passengers to reach the platform. Sidings were frequently built to facilitate a primary early use of Highland railways: the loading and off-loading of agricultural and heavy industrial goods, including livestock, timber and quarried stone.

Signalling Equipment

The single-tracked Highland lines made signalling equipment an important part of the construction process in the days of mechanical signalling. Stations and junctions were often isolated, so that attention was paid to making signal boxes comfortable and convenient for signalmen who might spend hours between each train coming through. Semaphore signalling was used on the early lines, but by the time the West Highland was built and opened (in 1894), the electric token system was available. In the 1980s, RETB (radio electronic token block) was introduced on the Highland lines.

Many of the original signal boxes were demolished, but some remain in use while still others have been converted into waiting rooms or even tourist accommodation. Some boxes have been listed for their architectural value, preventing their demolition. At Dunkeld & Birnam on the Highland Main Line, the 1919 Highland railway box still stands as a listed building: 'Brick with weatherboarding and multi-pane glazing to cabin accessed by timber forestair to half-gabled entrance porch outshot at upper level' (britishlistedbuildings. co.uk).

Railway Stations

Just under 100 of Scotland's 358 railway stations lie in the Highlands area as defined for this book. They range from the relatively busy hubs at Inverness, Aberdeen and Fort William, down to lonely stations isolated from any significant settlements, most notably on Rannoch Moor (West Highland) and along

Former signal box (listed) at Dunkeld & Birnam station (formerly 'Dunkeld').

the Far North Line. Like the lines, these stations (along with depots and sidings) were originally built by individual Highland companies – often financed by local landowners – but control eventually passed to British Rail and then, under privatization, to the UK infrastructure corporation, Network Rail. Since 2015, Network Rail (Scotland Route) has worked in 'a close working relationship' with Abellio ScotRail in managing the Scottish line infrastructure and stations.

The photo of Insch station sign, against an unusually azure sky, incorporates both the former British Rail (and Network Rail) red and white 'double arrow' and ScotRail branding. Transport Scotland has specific rules for station signage: 'The British Rail double arrow is the widely recognized symbol for all railway stations. As such, it should be retained on all road and street signage and as an identification mark at the entrance to ScotRail stations.'

Principal Depots

The principal depots for maintaining the ScotRail fleet are in the Central Belt, near Edinburgh (Haymarket depot) and Glasgow (three depots), but

Station sign for Insch showing the national rail logo (red symbol), and ScotRail/Scotland's Railway in blue livery.

there is also a yard at Inverness – the TMD (Traction Maintenance Depot) situated just outside Inverness station, past the Milburn Road junction. The depot helps to maintain the 'workhorse' Class 158 Express DMUs on Highland lines, together with carrying out checks on the Caledonian Sleeper trains.

Rolling Stock: Past to Present

Rolling stock on the Highland lines – locomotives, multiple units, passenger coaches and freight carriers – is documented in great detail in books dedicated to individual lines or railway companies (*see* Sources at the end of this book, and within the journey chapters), and this detail need not be reproduced here. Features of rolling stock development included:

- The manufacturing and maintenance, in the early days, of rolling stock by railway companies with rights to routes, such as Great North of Scotland and Highland Railway. Later, sub-contracting increased as the manufacturing industry became more concentrated, particularly around Glasgow
- Individual 'locomotive superintendents' were employed by the early companies to take personal charge of commissioning and/or designing the stock

Account had to be taken of the demands that an upland terrain would place on rolling stock, particularly locomotives: steep gradients, the power to haul heavy freight loads, fuel capacity for long journeys, and the likelihood of inclement weather affecting the track itself (especially snow and high winds). As summarized by the Highland Railway Society:

> Working the steep gradients of the main line, in particular, was always a challenge. Add strong winds and snow and the problems became even worse. The railway introduced the first 4-6-0s to the British Isles, commemorated in the preserved HR No.103 at the Glasgow Transport Museum.* http://www.hrsoc.org.uk/Railway.html
> * now Riverside Museum of Transport, Glasgow

In the later days of steam, a familiar sight on Highland tracks were the Stanier (or LMS) 'Black Five' locomotives, of which 842 were built, designed by William Stanier between 1934 and 1951 for LMS (London Midland & Scottish). Appropriately for mountain railways, some became known as 'hikers', as they carried what appeared to be backpacks of cylinders on top of the boiler engine. The oldest of

Locomotive HR103 (Highland Railway) at Riverside Museum, Glasgow. The first 4-6-0 in Britain, built in 1894. Above and behind, Glasgow & South West's No. 9 (Class 5, 0-6-0, 1917).

Class 43 (43168) 'InterCity' alongside Class 170 (170412, sadly missing its '7') at Pitlochry (Highland Main).

the surviving LMS Blacks is preserved by Strathspey Railway at Aviemore.

As elsewhere in Britain, under British Rail the transition took place in Scotland from steam to diesel or electric motive power from the 1950s onwards, while passenger carriages were upgraded and modernized, and freight moved towards enclosed containers rather than open wagons.

Most recently, between 2017 and 2019, ScotRail took delivery of a fleet of high-speed trains (HST) formerly in use by England's Great Western franchise; the refurbished HST work the long distance (Inter7City) routes from Edinburgh to Aberdeen (and on to Dyce). Power cars 43021 and 43132 were delivered to ScotRail in September 2017, and after

staff training, the first Inter7City service began in October 2018.

Also seen on the Scottish Highland Main Line since December 2019 have been high-speed, bi-modal (electric and diesel traction) multiple units branded for LNER (London–Inverness, the 'Highland Chieftain') as 'Azuma'. The units are assembled by Hitachi in England (Newton Aycliffe) under British Rail Class 800.

The ScotRail fleet under the Abellio franchise has, therefore, been through a period of transition (2017–2020) with HST (Class 43) and EMU (Class 380) arriving on the main lines. There are still seventy-eight 'Sprinter' DMUs: forty Express Sprinter (Class 158) and thirty-eight Super Sprinter

(Class 156) in service on Highland lines. Another workhorse has been the Class 170, of which Abellio had fifty-five sets, latterly reduced to thirty-four, running out of the company's major depot at Haymarket, Edinburgh.

The transition in 2019–2020 will see Class 153 Super Sprinter DMUs introduced on the West Highland, Kyle and Far North lines. Built in England in the late 1980s (as Class 155) to serve on suburban lines (maximum speed is 75mph), the 153s are single-coach units that can couple with various other Classes when necessary (including 156s and 158s). To suit usage of the Highland trains, carriages have been restructured to allow more space for bicycles and outdoor equipment.

Meanwhile, rail passengers in the Central Belt – particularly commuters – have enjoyed the introduction of Hitachi Class 385 on newly electrified lines.

Earliest Rail Companies in the Highlands

Appendix II provides a 'company family tree' through to the modern era, while Appendix III gives a more detailed timeline of line openings.

There was a flurry of activity in the mid-1840s, coinciding with the 'railway mania' that was infecting the investment community of Britain as a whole. The investments of that era will crop up in each of the following 'journey' chapters. Prior to that period, the Highlands were inevitably slower than the Lowlands to develop railways, the first – primitive – lines opening around Dundee and Perth, although the Grampian region benefited from numerous early lines, few of which would survive.

The most important factor in the Highlands in the early decades was that Scottish railway investors favoured reaching Inverness, the Highland capital, and then the northern Highlands, via the east coast and Aberdeen. This 'long way round' seems extraordinary to those who today take advantage of the straight run almost directly northwards (by rail or by road) into and through the Central Highlands, via Stirling and Perth, to reach Inverness (using the Main Line route, described in Chapter 4).

Great North of Scotland Railway (GNOS) developed out of Aberdeen as the main company in the Grampian region, while Scottish North Eastern Railway (SNER) crept northwards from the Central Belt in the 1850s. While GNOS was heading west, Inverness & Aberdeen Junction was heading east, and their lines would meet to create today's main Inverness–Aberdeen route (minus some station and junction closures). To reach Inverness more directly from the south, a Perth & Inverness company had its proposal rejected by Parliament, and permission for this direct line through the Cairngorms was not obtained until 1884. Instead, Inverness & Perth Junction built northwards from Dunkeld to Aviemore in the early 1860s, but reached Inverness circuitously via Forres on the Moray coast.

Today's Main Line, the direct line over the Cairngorms, was launched as Inverness & Aviemore Direct, but the full line was not completed until 1897 (by Highland, which had absorbed Inverness & Perth Junction). Components of the Main Line further south had been developed by Perth & Dunkeld, Scottish Midland Junction and Scottish Central.

Further north, the Duke of Sutherland's was a pioneer in the 1860s, connected to Dingwall and Inverness by Highland Railway, which much later (1897) completed the Dingwall–Kyle line. In the west, Oban had a cross-country line from 1880 (Callander & Oban, later lost), but the West Highland from Glasgow to Fort William (and Mallaig) was not completed until the last years of the old century.

The Highland Rail Network Today

Travelling by train in the Highlands entails joining one of eight routes, each detailed in the chapters that follow:

- The Highland Main Line, starting initially in either Glasgow or Edinburgh, passing through Perth (junction) to Inverness (junction). Important stations en route are Perth, Pitlochry and

Aviemore. ScotRail, LNER and Caledonian Sleeper work this line (or part of it), LNER's through services originating at London's King's Cross. This book focuses on the line starting at Perth

- The East Coast, from Edinburgh to Aberdeen, also shared by ScotRail and LNER (in part by CrossCountry and Caledonian Sleeper); this book focuses on stations north of Dundee, which include Arbroath, Montrose and Stonehaven
- The West Highland Line, starting at Glasgow Queen Street but with the emphasis of Highland coverage from Helensburgh to Fort William via Crianlarich and Tyndrum. (Two branches or 'extensions' from this line are treated as separate journeys in this book)
- Aberdeen to Inverness – the line mostly through the 'Grampian' region (Aberdeenshire, Moray and the Cairngorms National Park)
- The Far North Line from Inverness via Dingwall to Thurso and Wick on the north coast
- Three routes that were originally developed to reach the west coast of the Highlands: Inverness to Kyle of Lochalsh via Dingwall; Crianlarich (from a West Highland junction) to Oban; and Fort William to Mallaig

Lost Lines… and Preserving the Heritage

Each chapter of this book dedicated to a journey will include information about former railway lines in the Highlands that were lost in the twentieth century, most of them due to the Beeching cuts.

Arguments continue over how many of these would be viable today. For example, the Royal Deeside Line (closed in 1966: *see* Chapter 2), which was used by Queen Victoria, might have become a popular choice for both commuters to Aberdeen and twenty-first-century tourists visiting Balmoral Castle and the Cairngorm mountains. And the old cross-country, east–west line from Callander to Oban might have thrived in the modern era of tourism as the main Highland routes all run north to south.

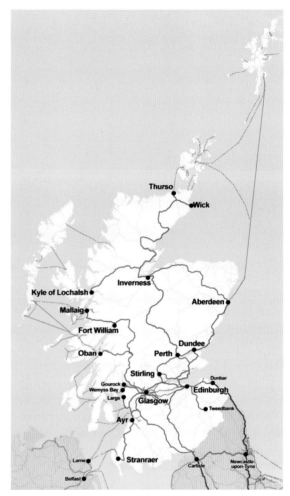

Scottish railway network in 2019. OPENSTREETMAP

The other 'lost lines' described will include:

- Banff, Macduff & Turriff Junction (1857–1966)
- Dunblane, Doune & Callander (1858–1965)
- Formartine & Buchan (1858–1966)
- Invergarry & Fort Augustus (1903–46)
- Montrose & Bervie (1865–1966)

Scotland as a whole has eighteen stretches of preserved railway, of which four are in the Highlands. The Deeside line has been revived (as Royal Deeside) since 1996, with a mile of track available from Milton of Crathes towards Banchory. Another

ScotRail service crossing Glenfinnan Viaduct, made famous in the Harry Potter movies. NORMAN MCNAB

revived name is that of Caledonian Railway (Brechin), in Angus, which runs excursions on 4 miles of line between Brechin and Bridge of Dun (on the previous line to Montrose).

The longest established preserved railway is the Strathspey, which uses part of the former line from Aviemore towards Grantown-on-Spey over 10 miles of track from Aviemore to Broomhill.

The 'Whisky Line' operates between Keith in Morar and Dufftown in Speyside for 11 miles. Further south, in Alford, Aberdeenshire, is the Grampian Transport Museum, close to which is a half-mile of narrow-gauge track based on the original Alford Valley Line, which connected Alford to Aberdeen via Kintore.

Perhaps the most important heritage service, however, runs not on a recreated line but on an existing line: Fort William to Mallaig. Sharing the whole of this 43-mile line with ScotRail, West Coast Railways operates steam journeys on a twice-daily summer service called *The Jacobite*, recalling the arrival at Glenfinnan of Bonnie Prince Charlie in 1745. Since the use of the Glenfinnan viaduct for filming Harry Potter movies, the viaduct has become even more famous around the world.

Mention must be made of volunteer organizations that help to maintain, or preserve, specific railway stations in the Highlands. A particularly active group is the Community Rail Partnership, responsible for the upkeep of stations on the Highland Main Line (https://www.highlandmainlinecrp.co.uk) – but this is just one example. Since 2016 there has been restoration work at Invergarry station (open until 1946 on the Invergarry–Fort Augustus line), including a museum and a short stretch of track. Many other Highland stations now play an active role in local tourism or culture, helping to enhance the image of train travel.

CHAPTER 2

Earliest Lines: The East Coast

As noted in the Preface, when defining the Scottish Highlands, the east coast and Grampians are included in the coverage of this book. This might cause the occasional Scottish eyebrow to be raised, but it would be impossible to grasp the development of railways in the northern half of Scotland without acknowledging the influence of the east coast and the Grampian region.

Commercial interests behind the building of railways on the east coast of Scotland were both profitable and diverse: the goods to be transported ranged from livestock, grain, timber and textiles to Aberdeenshire's famous granite, together with herring and other fish from the North Sea ports. And as elsewhere in Britain, the advantage of rail for delivering the mail was undeniable.

Chronologically, the earliest developments north of the Central Belt certainly took place on the east – and in Perthshire – and this was partly explained by the relative ease of building a railway along the mainly flat coastline of Angus and Aberdeenshire.

Early on, there was strong demand for transport

Modern view of the North Sea from the East Coast line: offshore wind-farm turbines instead of oil rigs and tankers.
ISTOCK.COM/STUSTOX

– passenger and freight – from this rich region, both agriculturally and industrially. However, two other factors came into play: early evidence of a 'race to the north', in the sense of opening a line all the way from England to Inverness; and, more unusually, the impetus supplied by royal approval.

1840–50 Railway Mania

In 1844, an orgy of railway promotion raged within the city... local citizens [were] determined to establish Aberdonian control over railways radiating for 100 miles out of the city.

North of Scotland, by John Thomas and David Turnock

In the broader context of early railways in Scotland as a whole, the south had inevitably led the way with its concentrations of population and industry. The first 'wagonways' appeared between Kilmarnock & Troon, Ayrshire (1812), between Monkland & Kirkintilloch, Strathclyde (1826) and Edinburgh & Dalkeith (1831), and they were initially horse-drawn. The 1830s and early 1840s brought steam traction,

regular passenger services and a proliferation of Lowland lines including Glasgow to Edinburgh and lines across the English border.

By 1850, two major companies had emerged in southern Scotland: North British and Caledonian, and they will crop up in the story of Highland railways as they expressed ambitions to extend northwards.

Smaller start-ups based on Tayside (serving Perth and Dundee) would also play their part. As early as 1831, a line inland from Dundee to the modest destination of Newtyle had been built, and Dundee had a coast line to Arbroath by 1838, both built by independent companies. Arbroath itself achieved a link inland (to Forfar, 1839).

Piecemeal investment by small joint stock companies with regional interests – Arbroath & Forfar, Montrose & Bervie, Scottish Midland Junction and others – held back development in the region until the inrush of money during 'rail mania'. With royalty providing the seal of approval for train travel, 'railway mania' was taking off across Britain in the 1840s. It has been suggested that the amount proposed for investing in railways during

Lochee West station, open 1861–1916 on Dundee & Newtyle. (Originally as 'Victoria' station, later as 'Camperdown'.)
SRPS

the 'mania', over £200 million, was in excess of Britain's entire gross domestic product. What is known for certain is that 272 Acts of Parliament involving railways were passed at the height of the speculation in 1846.

Aberdeen Railway was one of the companies with more substantial funding, building (or working) a line from Ferryhill (on the south of the city) down the coast to Montrose and inland to Brechin and Forfar (by 1850). But investment was also moving northwards from central Scotland, and in 1856, Aberdeen amalgamated with Scottish Midland Junction into the much larger Scottish North Eastern Railway (SNER), which was later able to gain even more dominance by absorbing two other lines: Dundee & Arbroath, and Perth, Almond Valley & Methven.

Royal Approval of 'The Finest Country in the World'

In the autumn of 1842, at the age of twenty-three but already in her fifth year on the throne, Queen Victoria paid her first visit to Scotland by ship and horse-drawn carriage. But it was crucial that she and her consort, Prince Albert, already favoured travel by train; earlier in the same year, Victoria had taken the first ever train journey by a British monarch:

I am quite charmed by it. By railroad from Windsor in half an hour, free from dust and heat.

Queen Victoria, letter to King Leopold of Belgium, her uncle, after her first train journey from Slough to Paddington, 13 June 1842

At Ballater station visitor centre, a reproduction of Queen Victoria's royal waiting room laid out for dinner with crystal and silver table settings.

The royal couple also favoured the Highlands enough to purchase Balmoral Castle as their summer holiday home, and this joint approval – of railways and of the Scottish Highlands – would help to pave the way for the East Coast Line (and the branch into the Dee valley, towards their castle).

As mentioned earlier, Aberdeen Railway had developed a terminus at Ferryhill, south Aberdeen, and it was from here that an inland line would run, to be known as the Deeside Railway (later, Royal Deeside as a heritage line). There was the usual 1840–50 gestation period, from the initial idea in 1848 to the line opening in 1853, but this came just in time to service the royal party.

> The solitude, the romance and wild loveliness of everything here, the absence of hotels and beggars, the independent simple people, who all speak Gaelic, all make beloved Scotland the proudest, finest country in the world.
>
> Queen Victoria's *Highland Journal* of
> 2 September 1869

Although Deeside was lost to Beeching, the impact of royal usage in its early days could not be under-estimated. What was good for their Queen was good for the British population, so royal usage would have helped promote the new form of transport to an initially wary populace.

Victoria's choice of the Highlands as her holiday destination had a deep significance for Britain. Since 1633, monarchs had generally eschewed visiting their subjects in Scotland – apart from a brief visit in 1822 by George IV – so Victoria and Albert's use of Balmoral had a crucial influence on national goodwill and the early development of tourism from England.

The 'lost line' of Royal Deeside is described at the end of this chapter.

A Tale of Two Bridges

By the 1860s, railways in the north-east of Scotland had been strengthened by amalgamation, more solid investment, and the arrival of 'national' companies such as North British and Caledonian (which extended its reach considerably with the absorption of SNER in 1866). Inland lines and some coastal connections were important in the early development of railways in this region, starting in the 1830s, but it was not until the 1850s that medium- and long-distance through-routes became a reality.

But a long-term problem of geography remained: the estuaries (or firths) of the River Tay and River Forth, which cut across Scotland from west to east to reach the North Sea. On the Tay estuary, ferries were consigned to history with the construction of the first rail bridge in 1879. Tragically, within two

Railway bridge (1887) over the firth of the River Tay from Wormit to Dundee (south to north). Note the stumps of the piers from the previous bridge that collapsed on 28 December 1879. iSTOCK. COM/ALANFIN

years the bridge collapsed during a storm, taking with it a North British train from Edinburgh, whose seventy-five passengers and crew were lost in the icy waters of the Tay. Nevertheless, a replacement bridge was built by 1887 and continues in use today.

The Tay Bridge disaster of 1879 led to rigorous design and testing procedures for the new bridge over the Tay, and even more so for the bridge over the Forth. Brought into use in 1890, and a working bridge ever since, the Forth Rail Bridge was massive enough to qualify as a 'wonder of the world' in its time, with its 53,000 tonnes of steel and 6.5 million rivets. It has been an inspiration for photographers – and postcards – for more than a century.

The East Coast: Station by Station

A Historic Journey from Edinburgh to Aberdeen
Although this is a book about Scottish Highland railways, it would be incomplete without some mention of the Lowland stations where passengers for destinations such as Aberdeen, Inverness or Fort William begin their long journeys.

The line running close to the east coast of Scotland forms part of the line that stretches from London's King's Cross to Edinburgh, the most frequent stops in northern England including York and Newcastle, before continuing to either Aberdeen (the Northern Lights service) or Inverness (the Highland Chieftain). The East Coast franchise has been operated by London North Eastern Railway (LNER), controlled by the UK government, since 2018, prior to which it was operated by Virgin Trains.

Taking a journey from Edinburgh to Aberdeen, there is a choice of services by ScotRail's Inter7City HST or by LNER, but this journey will choose the 'stopping' ScotRail service in order to describe the main stations called at on a typical run. (A route from Glasgow to Aberdeen is possible, of course, but Glasgow as a departure point for the Highlands will be outlined in Chapter 4, 'Scotland's Backbone: the Highland Main Line'.)

The 'all stations' services on a typical journey in 2019 on this route would still have been hauled by the familiar Class 170 Turbostar, a DMU workhorse on ScotRail's medium-haul routes. Many 170s are due to be replaced, but Abellio ScotRail was still leasing thirty-nine of them in 2019 for operations out of the Haymarket depot near Edinburgh.

Edinburgh Waverley

Edinburgh Waverley station is named after the 'Waverley' series of novels by Sir Walter Scott (1771–1832), a proud son of the city, although 'Edinburgh' also suffices as the station name. The distinctive tower of the five-star Balmoral Hotel (originally the North British) sits high above the station; the clocks on the tower were (and still are) set a few minutes fast so passengers would make their trains on time. A wall plaque in Waverley station commemorates Sir Nigel Gresley (1876–1941), 'born in this city', Britain's most famous steam locomotive designer.

Heading westwards from Waverley, there are views up to the castle and then the first port of call is the original terminus of the Glasgow–Edinburgh line (1842), Haymarket station, rebuilt and reopened in 2014. Then come two other twenty-first-century stations, Edinburgh Park (2003) and Edinburgh Gateway (2016), to the west of the city, before the Aberdeen train embarks northwards on the historic crossing over the Forth Rail Bridge. Crossing into the county (or 'kingdom') of Fife, the line passes through a flat landscape including seven stations primarily serving commuters to Edinburgh.

The last stop in Fife, Leuchars, although not yet in the Highlands, has an enduring significance for Scotland's rail network. From this station, buses depart every few minutes for Newburgh or Dundee and, critically, to St Andrews, which was cut off from the rail network during the Beeching cuts. Leuchars itself was renowned for its Royal Air Force base from 1911 to 2015; the extensive soldiers' barracks remain, surrounding the train station. An odd piece of railway history occurred at Leuchars in 1913 when the station burned to the ground, with suffragettes suspected of arson.

Ten minutes out of Leuchars elapse before the train crosses the Tay Bridge, where thoughts inevitably turn to the disaster of 1879: from the shores of the Tay, the stumps of the stone piers that supported

Dundee station, rebuilt in 2018 as part of the city's Waterfront project. Note the Pendeen pebble seats supplied by Barrell Sculpture ('a stunning alternative to traditional seating').

the first rail bridge can still be seen. The city of Dundee comes into view from the rail bridge, and the train enters its station almost immediately after crossing the river, on a track running parallel to the line from Perth in the west.

Dundee

Modern Dundee is unrecognizable from the industrial city, which had several competing stations in the first century of railways here; the dock area – Central Waterfront – has been transformed with the addition of the Victoria & Albert Museum of Design (opened in 2018). The new multi-storey station includes a Sleeperz Hotel on its upper floors, and state-of-the-art features such as Sheffield stands for 120 bicycles. The glass frontage can be lit up in different colours for special events during the year.

Dundee's Early Rail Connections

Once the city of 'jam, jute and journalism', now the 'city of discovery', Scotland's fourth largest city (population *c.* 150,000) hosted some of Scotland's earliest railways. Dundee & Newtyle (just 10 miles long) opened in 1831 using one of the first steam locomotives seen in Scotland, primarily for freight at a time of boom in the region's agricultural and industrial output. This purpose was typified by the fact that, as with termini on many early railways, Newtyle was merely a railhead terminus near a small village.

During the rest of the 1830s, short connections were made from Newtyle to Coupar Angus and to Glamis (the village next to Glamis Castle, childhood home of the Queen Mother, Elizabeth Bowes-Lyon). But of more significance for the future was Dundee & Arbroath (1838, initially with a very wide gauge, 5ft 6in), which evolved in the mid-1840s – the 'rail mania' time – into part of a growing network across Angus. Within Dundee, this meant building a rail link between Dundee & Arbroath's station in the east, and Dundee & Perth's station in the west of the city.

By 1871 there was also a Dundee & Forfar line, but independent operators in the region had been absorbed by companies moving northwards towards the Highlands: Scottish Central Railway (Stirling–Perth and Dundee–Perth), later absorbed by the even larger Caledonian, and the giant North British, which set up 'North British, Arbroath & Montrose' as a subsidiary to achieve its Edinburgh–Aberdeen ambition, using the Tay Bridge.

Stations within the Dundee Commuter Belt

From Dundee, the east coast line passes through a series of stations serving towns within the Dundee commuter belt, albeit towns that retain pride in their individuality. The gentrified former port of Broughty Ferry can claim to host Scotland's longest surviving railway station, having been established (in buildings modified since) on the Dundee & Arbroath in 1838. Balmossie station (or rather, a halt) was a suburban addition in 1962, but Monifieth also dated back to 1838: its original building on the eastbound platform was dismantled for display at the Glasgow Garden Festival of 1988, and was then (in 2000) incorporated into the new station at Birkhill on the Boness & Kinneil heritage line.

Barry Links (opened in 1851; it was just 'Barry' until April 2019) achieved dubious fame in 2017/18 by becoming Britain's least used station, according to the Office of Rail & Road statistics, with only fifty-two passengers arriving or departing (*see* Appendix IV, station usage statistics). A nearby feature is the MOD's Barry Buddon artillery range dating back to 1850: a Buddon Siding existed from an unconfirmed date to closure before 1957. Not many more passengers are bound for, or start their journeys, at the next station, Golf Street (added in 1960), but this is hardly surprising, given that both stations are called at only twice a day.

Carnoustie

In contrast to these stations, Carnoustie is used heavily when its famous links course hosts tournaments such as The Open in 2018, when Francesco Molinari became the first Italian to hold the claret jug prize. Previous winners – in years when Carnoustie hosted The Open and attracted users of its stations, both Golf Street and Carnoustie – included Tommy Armour (1931), Ben Hogan (1953), Gary Player (1968), Tom Watson (1975), Scotland's Paul Lawrie (1999) and Pádraig Harrington (2007).

From Carnoustie to Arbroath the line hugs the low-lying coastline for 7 miles, affording excellent views over sandy beaches to the North Sea.

Arbroath

As noted in the Dundee profile above, Arbroath was important in early railway history, as well as being famous more generally in Scottish history for its 'Declaration' of 1320: this was a letter to the Pope – later called the Declaration of Arbroath – that was ordered by King Robert ('the Bruce') and signed by thirty-nine earls and barons in the now ruined Arbroath Abbey. The Declaration was the king's plea for Scotland to be recognized in Christian Europe as an independent country.

All Aboard! Arbroath Station

A station called Arbroath Lady Loan, closer to the sea front, pre-dated the current station, as did the nearby site of Arbroath Catherine Street. As in other Highland settlements – Aberdeen, Dundee, Crianlarich – this was because early independent lines had separate stations. In this town, the lines were

GOLF BY TRAIN

The early origins of golf are disputed, but it was popular enough in Scotland for King James II (1430–60) to ban it because it distracted fighting men from practising their archery skills. Leith Links, Musselburgh and St Andrews' Royal & Ancient Club (R&A) all lay claim to founding the modern game, but the R&A took the lead in formalizing the rules of the game, and continues to administer it worldwide today (except in the USA and Mexico).

The nineteenth-century growth of golf and the railways went hand in hand. Before the motor car, transporting oneself with clubs and suitable clothing for golf was facilitated by the train, and railways often went through undeveloped coastal land that was also suitable for links courses. As early as 1915, Caledonian Railway had a map published that promoted over 260 golf courses reachable on its network. Caledonian built the Gleneagles Hotel with a station (still open today) dedicated to it; the hotel's championship course hosted the Ryder Cup in 2014 and the Solheim Cup in 2019.

The Ayrshire coast has a particular concentration of golf courses, including Royal Troon, Trump Turnberry and Prestwick, where the first twelve Open Championships (1860–72) were held. The railway line leaving Prestwick Town station abuts the first hole at Prestwick, which is named 'Railway' (as are the eleventh at Troon and the ninth at Carnoustie).

Arbroath station: the busy forecourt in the early twentieth century. SRPS

brought here in 2009, having been declared superfluous to the town's newly built Abbeygate shopping centre. Also on the station wall is a plaque commemorating 'Matthew B Kerr (1943–2006), Proprietor of Scotland's Oldest Miniature Railway'. Still a family business, Kerr's Miniature was founded in 1935 on Arbroath's West Links Park.

Leaving Arbroath

Leaving Arbroath, today's line heads inland, bypassing the suburb (and former village) of St Vigeans, which gave its name to an important junction in the 1880s (*see* panel below: The North British Moves Northwards), and then passing three former halts, all closed in 1930: Letham Grange (known for its golf club), Cauldcots and Inverkeilor, whose 1881 signal box still stands. Running closer towards the coast again, a steel viaduct had to be built over the river running into Lunan Bay, the seaside village also having its own station to 1930.

After Lunan Bay – and more views over the North Sea – comes a major geographical feature of the area

Dundee & Arbroath (1838) and Arbroath & Forfar (1839, later on the line from Forfar to Aberdeen). A tramway was built to connect the stations.

More services to and from Arbroath and Dundee (not just Aberdeen trains) have been added since 2018; the introduction of new Class 385 (electric) trains in Central Scotland freed up DMUs for use on the east coast 'commuter' journeys.

Long-distance services also pause for one minute at Arbroath. Within the capacious station can be viewed a Declaration of Arbroath mural

THE NORTH BRITISH MOVES NORTHWARDS: NBA&M

In its early years, the North British (founded 1844 in Edinburgh) had its focus on the south – linking up with English lines to the Scottish border at Berwick and Carlisle, and the west, Edinburgh–Glasgow – but by the 1860s the company was expanding northwards. Absorption of Edinburgh & Northern added services to Perth and Dundee in 1862, and eight years later the prospectus for North British, Arbroath & Montrose proposed a line that would help North British achieve its ambition of running long-distance services from Aberdeen all the way to the Scottish Borders.

The Tay Bridge, funded by North British, created a through-rail route from Fife to Dundee and beyond, although the dramatic collapse of the first bridge in 1879 meant that restoration of the service waited until the second bridge was completed in 1887. By then, the Forth Bridge – one-third backed by North British – had been under construction for five years, and its opening in 1890 created the long, continuous railway line that now runs down the east coast of Britain.

Completion of the NBA&M was delayed by having to rebuild the South Esk Viaduct, designed by Sir Thomas Bouch, the design engineer behind the ill-fated Tay Bridge. (Bouch was replaced by Sir William Arrol, whose other projects included the second Tay Bridge, the Forth Rail Bridge, the Caledonian Railway Bridge on the River Clyde in Glasgow, and Tower Bridge on the River Thames in London.) So the NBA&M, although given its royal assent in 1871, did not open to the public until 1883. By then, the line included the amalgamated Montrose & Bervie, opened in 1865.

Goods train crossing North Water Bridge Viaduct (Montrose & Bervie line 1865–1951). SRPS

(and, therefore, a challenge to railway construction) in the shape of the Montrose Basin, an inland lake with a wide outlet – the river South Esk – into the sea. Two viaducts of 1881 are crossed: the Rossie and the South Esk, the first of these built with seventeen arches (300 yards long), although drainage and infilling meant that water is only crossed a part of the way. The South Esk, built using iron piers and steel-latticed girders, is the more dramatic, with its fourteen spans and total length of nearly 500 yards.

Montrose

Like Arbroath, Montrose shares significance in Scottish history with an early historic role in railway development. For the general historian, the name itself conjures up images of the debonair, charismatic seventeenth-century warrior known simply as 'Montrose' ('Montrose' was 1st Marquess, James Graham, 1612–50, a military leader who took part on both sides of the civil war in Scotland in the mid-seventeenth century; he started out supporting the Covenanters, allied against the imposition of Charles I's English church liturgy, but later switched to the Royalist side). However, the town's role in rail was more modest. Montrose & Bervie was initiated as a local line in 1865, but eventually became part of grander plans initiated by Great North of Scotland and the mighty North British.

Montrose station (1883) sits next to the Basin, which is preserved by Scottish Wildlife Trust as the tidal home of over 80,000 migratory birds. An earlier Montrose station (1848) was connected to Aberdeen Railway's south-running line, while yet another was the 1865 terminus of Montrose & Bervie, acquired by North British.

Kinnaber Junction and the Race to the North

Out of Montrose, the East Coast line veers inland once more, and after a mile it passes the village of Hillside, tunnelling under Kinnaber Road. The former Kinnaber Junction here was famous in the 1890s as the culmination point of the 'race to the north' (*see* panel). 'Dismtd rly' (dismantled railway) on the Ordnance Survey maps indicates the line of the cutting that was taken by Caledonian's 'Strathmore' line to reach Kinnaber Junction from Perth via Forfar.

Caledonian had completed its 'Strathmore' route from Perth through Angus and southern Aberdeenshire, with a junction at Forfar (a strategic town, no longer connected to rail), then running on to meet Aberdeen Railway. Companies absorbed by Caledonian along the way included Scottish Midland Junction, Scottish Central and Scottish North Eastern, the last of which was active within Aberdeen city, working with Great North of Scotland.

North British, meanwhile, had used the North British, Arbroath & Montrose venture, together with its financing of the Tay Bridge (twice) and then the Forth Bridge (opened in 1890), to become a company of choice for long-distance travel on the east coast. To complicate matters, North British also had running powers, granted by Parliament, over some Caledonian lines (to present a simple picture of this

complex part of the East Coast line, the genesis of Aberdeen Railway – building southwards – will be described in the profile of the city itself, below).

The Caledonian line from Strathmore survived until its Beeching closure (1967), which is slightly surprising in that it was a mostly rural line after Perth (on the Highland Main), apart from serving Coupar Angus and Forfar, while the coastal line was getting busier in anticipation of the North Sea oil boom.

After Kinnaber, the finishing line of the 'race to the north', both the original and modern lines become one, working its way inland to Marykirk and Laurencekirk rather than following the coast through Inverbervie (once connected by a branch line from Montrose, between 1865 and 1966). The line serves the villages of The Mearns, an area formerly classified as the county of Kincardineshire but now part of Aberdeenshire.

Crossing the River North Esk over an impressive, thirteen-span viaduct (1849) at Marykirk – where there was a station from 1849 until 1956 – one in three ScotRail daily services stop at Laurencekirk, which reopened in 2009 having been lost to

BACKGROUND TO THE 'RACE TO THE NORTH'

Competition on long-distance routes from the south to the north of Scotland had intensified from the 1870s as larger, amalgamated competitors emerged. They absorbed regional and local companies, or leased their lines across central and north-east Scotland, so that by 1890, two long-distance forces had emerged in terms of reaching Aberdeen from the south: Caledonian and North British.

The 'race to the north' competition of the mid-1890s was a public relations and marketing coup more akin to twentieth-century marketing than that of the nineteenth century. The imagination of long-distance train users – in those days, mostly the well heeled – was captured by the race to Aberdeen from London (Euston or King's Cross) using either the eastern or western routes (the franchises today continue that tradition as InterCity East Coast and InterCity West Coast).

On 1 August 1888, the groups of companies (English and Scottish) competing on these routes challenged each other to reduce their London–Edinburgh times from nine to eight hours. Peace was resumed until 1895, by which time the Forth Bridge was open, giving the East an advantage over the longer 'race to the north', beyond Edinburgh to Aberdeen. Another temporary display of bravado took place in August, when the West Coast 'made a supreme effort, taking their train over the 540 miles from London to Aberdeen at 63.3mph' (*Oxford Companion to British Railway History*, quoting O.S. Nock's *Railway Race to the North*, 1958).

Although entertaining, the 'races' did not have a lasting effect on the railways due to the sacrifices that had to be made: drivers' hours and conditions, the weight of the trains themselves, limiting the number of stops, and having to 'race' in the dead of night – none of these providing a convenience for passengers or freight. Even so, between 1850 and 1900, journey time from London was cut from 12.5 to 7.5 hours. Branding for services such as *Scotch Express* and *Flying Scotsman* illustrated the marketing ploy of the era and generally helped to promote the idea of long-distance train travel.

Under British Rail (1948–1994) the race became irrelevant, but since privatization and the separate franchising of east and west 'coastal' routes, competition has returned.

Beeching in 1967. Local commuters had campaigned for a decade to reopen the station, which was used by 64,000 passengers in its first year, far more than anticipated. The original stone-built station building (1849) was retained, refurbished and repainted in white with pretty splashes of light blue and crimson.

Stonehaven

Between Laurencekirk and Stonehaven, the next current stop, there were once stations at Fordoun, Drumlithie and New Mill Offset until pre-Beeching rationalization in the 1950s. Today there is a fourteen-minute run through this rural area to the coast at genteel Stonehaven, with its picturesque harbour and beach.

Stonehaven station is, in fact, a thirty-minute stroll from the centre of town, Aberdeen Railway having decided it unnecessary to reach the harbour.

Of all the stations on the Aberdeen Railway line of the 1840s and 1850s, Stonehaven retains most of the original features, including a signal box and canopied station buildings.

The town of Stonehaven itself has benefited from its rail links and proximity to Aberdeen, especially since the 'oil rush' of the 1970s, with gentrification and high property prices very apparent. Expansion westwards means that the modern town now envelops the formerly isolated station. Just to the south (off the railway line) is the area's most famous historic attraction, Dunnottar Castle. To the north, the line leaving Stonehaven up the coast crosses over the north-eastern extremity of the geological feature known as the Highland Boundary Fault. (Of interest in railway terms is that the Fault starts in the south-west at the coast near Helensburgh, which is also the coastal location for the start of the West Highland Line.)

Stonehaven: the town clustered around the harbour and Stonehaven Bay. ISTOCK.COM/IWETA0077

After Stonehaven, the pace picks up for the twenty-two-minute final run into Aberdeen, non-stop through the station in the dormitory town of Portlethen. This final run offers splendid views of the North Sea at Muchalls (the station closed in 1950) and Cove Bay (1956). (In 2019, NESTRANS was studying the possibility of reopening up to three stations south of Aberdeen, including one at Cove.)

There is a swerve inland at Nigg Bay, where a £350m deep-water harbour project was due to be completed in 2021, enabling the largest cruise liners to dock at Aberdeen. The line then runs alongside the industrial estate in the Torry area before crossing the river on the Dee Viaduct (1850) and making its way into Aberdeen station. In total, this makes it a three-hour journey from Edinburgh, including a change at Arbroath.

Aberdeen: The City and its Railway History

Visitors arriving in Aberdeen by train are immediately confronted by all the elements of a modern, thriving, commercial city and port: a great contrast to the bucolic run along the North Sea coast and through rolling, rural hills earlier on the journey north.

The area around the station, as with so many modern urban stations, is unprepossessing but functional: it adjoins the modern Union Square shopping centre of 2009, beyond which lie the docks area where vessels connected to oil and fishing arrive, together with the ferries to Orkney and Shetland.

Aberdeen is Scotland's third largest city (with a population of 208,000) after Glasgow and Edinburgh. The ancient capital of Grampian, the city already had a rich history long before North Sea oil and gas reserves were discovered in the 1960s, eventually turning the city into 'Europe's oil capital'. Tourism is also developing: large cruise ships will dock at Aberdeen from 2020, and the City Centre Masterplan (2015–2020) has transformed attractions such as Provost Skene's House (seventeenth century), the art gallery and Marischal College, all of which are in walking distance from the station. (Transport is needed to get to Old Aberdeen, in the north of the city, home to St Machar's Cathedral and the original university, founded in 1495.)

With high-speed services entering and leaving the city (by both ScotRail and LNER), the modern railway network is very different from its nineteenth-century origins. Two companies, both with misnomers for names, pioneered rail in and around Aberdeen. They were Great North of Scotland

Aberdeen station with Highland Railway No. 2 'Aldourie', 2-2-2, Raigmore class. SRPS

Aberdeen station entrance, dwarfed by the modern shopping centre (Union Square).

(GNOS) – Aberdeen is, in fact, only halfway 'north' from the Central Belt to Scotland's northernmost tip, served by Far North Line – and Aberdeen Railway, whose first terminus, Ferryhill, was just as far from the centre of Aberdeen as GNOS's Kittybrewster terminus.

The detailed development of GNOS will be reserved for the next chapter – covering Grampian railways to the north and west of Aberdeen – because that was the eventual focus of the Great North: to provide railways to coastal towns in Grampian, and to reach Inverness. Within Aberdeen, however, a starting point was needed, and GNOS chose the suburb of Kittybrewster – nowadays engulfed by expansion of the university and public housing along the A98, or Great Northern Road – for its terminus.

Opened in 1854, Kittybrewster's line ran northeastwards – on the track used today – through stations (now closed) at Woodside and Buxburn on the way to Keith (and an eventual connection with Highland Railway's line from Inverness). GNOS did build a station closer to the city centre, called Waterloo (opened in 1855), but this was half a mile from the city centre terminus of the southbound Aberdeen Railway at Guild Street. Notoriously, the two competing companies refused to make life easy for passengers or freight transferring between stations – by horse-drawn 'omnibus' – so much so that questions were raised in Parliament. A joint station was eventually opened at Guild Street in 1867.

Aberdeen Railway

Aberdeen Railway was given its royal assent as early as 1830, but its gestation coincided, in the era of 'rail mania' investment, with the start of the Great North between 1845 and 1855. As recorded earlier in this chapter, principal stations were opened at Stonehaven, Laurencekirk and Montrose; the later 1850s and 1860s brought a complexity of deals ending with Aberdeen Railway as part of Scottish North Eastern, which meant that trains from Aberdeen continued on to Arbroath and Dundee or Perth (and thence via other operators to the Central Belt).

All Aboard: Aberdeen Station

The station where passengers alight today is the only railway station in Aberdeen, which at various times had other termini at Kittybrewster, Ferryhill and Guild Street. The first 'joint' station for rail companies serving Aberdeen opened in 1867 but was completely rebuilt during and after World War I.

No longer fit for purpose by the dawn of the twenty-first century, the station underwent a major overhaul and reopened in 2009 as part of the Union Square development incorporating transport, retail, leisure and hotels. (There are over fifty shops, a dozen restaurants, a Cineworld multiplex and a Jurys Inn, and Union Square bus terminal.) Much of the land used was an old goods yard; the original station building – unusually for Aberdeen, in sandstone rather than granite – was retained.

More recent improvements have included re-roofing and an extension of the site (by demolishing the Atholl House office block) into another public square, surrounded by student housing, another hotel and more shops.

Lost Lines and Heritage on the East Coast

Royal Deeside Railway

Closed in 1966 under Beeching, the Deeside Railway towards Balmoral ran originally from Ferryhill, 5 miles south of Aberdeen centre, for 55 miles to Ballater, following the course of the River Dee directly westwards.

Ferryhill (from 1853), Aberdeen Railway's first terminus in the city, was replaced within two years by the Guild Street terminus, but its junction preserved its place in local railway history as the first terminus for the Deeside Railway. The Ferryhill Railway Heritage Trust, established in 2007, has restored a turntable next to Duthie Park for use by steam locomotives sharing the main line.

At its peak there were more than twenty stops and halts on the Deeside line, the main towns served being Culter, Banchory, Aboyne and Ballater. It was planned to extend the line as far as Braemar, but the royal family objected to the line running through its estate. (A traction engine offered transport by road from Ballater, and a terminal station – now a private house – was built by Great North of Scotland in Braemar.)

The Royal Deeside Railway heritage group has revived a one-mile length out of its base at Milton of

Private house in Braemar (with the author), originally meant for the station on Deeside Line from Ballater (not completed).

Visitor centre at Ballater, Deeside, on the site of the former station, completed in 2018, on a snowy day in 2019. Note the cycle racks and the 'Information' sign.

Crathes, a collection of restored buildings including a railway station, brasserie and antique shops. The company offers a range of heritage rolling stock and a rebuilt station at Milton, including a tearoom in a carriage. The old line was closed in 1966 and the track was lifted in 1972.

At Aboyne, the substantial station building (built in 1896) now offers shops and a café with an external plaque commemorating the following:

> ...the extension of the Deeside Railway from Banchory to Aboyne on 2 December 1859. Her Majesty Queen Victoria first travelled to Aboyne by train on 8 August 1860.
>
> (The Great North of Scotland Railway Association)

The station building at Ballater survived until a devastating fire in 2016, but reopened as a visitor attraction – including a royal waiting room – in 2018.

The original waiting room (created in 1886) was graced with visits not only by Victoria and Albert but by their eminent guests at Balmoral, such as the Shah of Persia and Czar Nicholas II, who benefited from electric lighting and, as described on the Deeside Railway website, the 'fabulous royal toilet!'.

Caledonian Railway

Further down the East Coast, 'Caledonian Railway' obtained a Light Railway Order in 1993 to run excursions on an old line from Bridge of Dun to Brechin. Volunteers are drawn from the Brechin Railway Preservation Society, formed in 1979. (At the time, BR was still using the line from Brechin as far as Kinnaber Junction, for freight traffic.) The group owns more than twenty locomotives (eight steam, the rest heritage diesel from 1949–1962), of which two steam models are operational for excursions, both built by Andrew Barclay Sons & Co of Kilmarnock (no. 1863 built in 1926, and 22107 built in 1941). Excursions have enticing names such as Steam Sunday, Whisky Whistler and Easter Eggspress. The Brechin Society won a Queen's Award for Voluntary Service in 2019, its fortieth anniversary.

Brechin and Bridge of Dun, no longer connected to modern rail, were the last stations at the southern end of the original Aberdeen Railway route, but by 1866 – when Caledonian Railway took over the line – they were also connected to Montrose, Forfar and Perth inland, and Arbroath and Dundee along the coast. This necessitated trains passing through the curiously named junction of Friockheim (pronounced 'Free Come' and meaning 'home of heather').

Services on the East Coast of Scotland

In 2019, ScotRail operated the following services to Aberdeen from the south (timetable 19 May–14 December):

* Edinburgh (Waverley) to Aberdeen. Mon.–Sat.: Eleven daily, all stopping at Leuchars, Dundee, Arbroath. Sun.: Four daily. Other services requiring change at Dundee or Arbroath
* Glasgow Queen Street to Aberdeen. Mon.–Sat.: Fifteen daily via Stirling, Perth, Dundee, Arbroath. Other services requiring change at Perth or Dundee. Sun.: Ten daily
* From Aberdeen, connecting services for Dyce and Inverurie were advertised in the timetable up to 18 May but removed from the May–December timetable, due to revisions of the Aberdeen–Inverness timings

LNER had four daily services from London through to Aberdeen, stopping at (for example) Edinburgh 14.29, Leuchars 15.33, Dundee 15.46 and Arbroath 16.04.

Caledonian Sleeper (by Serco): Not advertised in ScotRail timetable but the nightly (except Saturday) 20.30 from London Euston stops at Leuchars, Dundee, Carnoustie, Arbroath, Montrose, Stonehaven and Aberdeen (arr. 7.39).

CrossCountry (franchise by Arriva) operates to 120 British stations including a daily through train from Plymouth (dep. 9.25) via Bristol, Birmingham, Leeds, York, Newcastle (and intervening English stations), Edinburgh (18.11), several Fife stations, principal east coast stations and arriving Aberdeen at 20.48. Also a daily service departing Plymouth requiring a change at Dundee for Aberdeen.

Sources for the East Coast Line

(*See also* Sources chapter at the end of this book for general sources.)

The History of the Railways of the Scottish Highlands (series 1977–1990):
Originally published by David & Charles, now from House of Lochar, Isle of Colonsay
3. Vallance, H.A., *The Great North of Scotland Railway*

Great North of Scotland Railway Association (publisher):
Jackson, D., *Royal Deeside's Railway: Aberdeen to Ballater* (1999)
Jones, K.G., T*he Railways of Aberdeen: 150 Years of History* (2000)

Jones, R., *A History of the East Coast Main Line* (Crowood Press 2017)

Simmons, J., *The Victorian Railway* (Thames & Hudson 1991)

Thomas, J. and Turnock, D., *A Regional History of the Railways of Great Britain Vol 15: The North of Scotland* (David & Charles 1989)

Internet (www.)

Caledonian Railway (Brechin)
(caledonianrailway.co.uk)

CrossCountry by Arriva
(crosscountrytrains.co.uk)

Great North of Scotland Railway Association
(gnsra.org.uk)

LNER: London North Eastern Railway
(lner.co.uk)

NESTRANS: North East Scotland Transport Partnership

(nestrans.org.uk)
Railscot.co.uk – primary resource for Scottish railway information

ScotRail
(ScotRail.co.uk) – official website of Abellio franchise

scot-rail
(scot-rail.co.uk) – Scotland's online rail enthusiast community

CHAPTER 3

Mid-Nineteenth-Century Developments: the Grampian Region

In Chapter 2, our story left the Highland railways at the city of Aberdeen, which had been connected to the south and east by 1850 (by Aberdeen Railway, Scottish North Eastern – later an extension northwards of Caledonian – and the northwards push of North British). Already, however, there were moves afoot to connect Aberdeen with the other great Highland city (then considered a town),

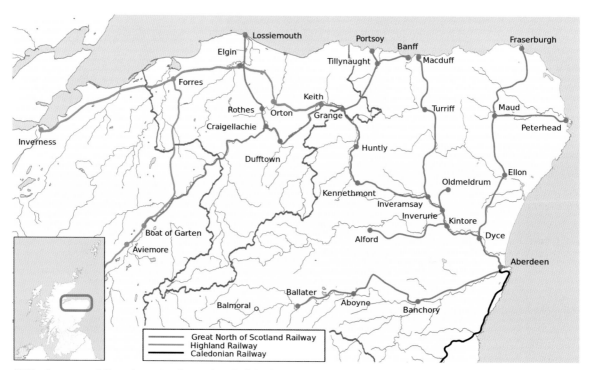

1867 railway map of Grampian region showing lines built by Great North of Scotland, Highland and Caledonian companies. Only Aberdeen–Inverness remains. WIKIMEDIA COMMONS

Rothes station (1858–1968) seen from the south in the 1960s, on the former Morayshire Line. Nothing remains of the station buildings today.
SRPS

Inverness, which meant building in a north-westerly direction.

Great North of Scotland (GNOS) was the first to tackle this task, although, as the century progressed, a joint effort would be needed for the Aberdeen–Inverness link to be completed: two lines, developed westwards by GNOS and eastwards by Inverness & Nairn – a founder member of what would become the extensive Highland Railway.

In addition to describing the Aberdeen–Inverness line – the only railway left in Grampian today, barring heritage services – this chapter also relates the mid-century history of other railways in the Grampian region. For today's uninformed observer, a surprising number of separate lines and branches once connected the towns and villages of prosperous Grampian.

Early 'Grampian' Lines and the Importance of Whisky

The 'rail mania' investments of 1845 described in Chapter 2 were not restricted to the big cities such as Dundee and Aberdeen. The Grampian terrain was relatively easy, following coastlines and river valleys; rail routes were developed quickly to connect otherwise isolated towns and villages dependent on farming or fishing; and there was plentiful produce from land and sea to be transported in bulk.

Surveys in various parts of Grampian took place in the early 1840s, and as early as 1846, royal assent was received for Morayshire Railway: the 'shire' in the county name was eventually dropped, and today's Moray is an extended local authority region including former Elginshire.

The first section built was the modest 5-mile run from the county town of Elgin – technically, a city – northwards to the coast at Lossiemouth. Delivering fish was enough to justify this early investment, but another need for freight haulage in the region was the whisky industry. The Speyside region's many distilleries are concentrated in an area south of Elgin, which encompasses Rothes (four distilleries operating today), Dufftown ('Rome was built on seven hills, Dufftown stands on seven stills'), Charlestown of Aberlour and Craigellachie, home of The Macallan and the Speyside Cooperage for supplying the oak casks. The target of Morayshire from the earliest was therefore to extend south of Elgin to Craigellachie.

The investors in Morayshire knew full well from the earliest discussions that other companies would hope to build a main line from Aberdeen to Inverness, and connecting to this would justify local branches. So a line from Rothes was built to a junction at the village of Orton, midway between Elgin and Keith, justifying the extension from Rothes to Craigellachie. This extension took place in 1858, a seminal year in which the main lines from Aberdeen (GNOS) and Inverness (Inverness & Aberdeen

WHISKY AND THE HIGHLAND RAILWAYS

The arrival of rail in the nineteenth century was convenient for transporting the necessary barley, oak casks (barrels) and bottles for producing whisky, although the prime ingredient – water – was delivered naturally by the burns (streams) flowing into the distilleries, to be turned into whisky (*uisge beatha*, or 'water of life', in Gaelic).

Always a key part of the Scottish economy, its whisky – called Scotch only outside the country – has grown massively as an export product, leading to distilleries opening up, rather than closing down as they used to. There are now over 130 of them, divided across five official regions: Speyside crams in over 100, but the Highland region tops the volume of production. Smaller whisky-producing regions are Lowland, Islay and Campbeltown.

Early distilling was a cottage industry, but taxation in the eighteenth century 'drove the distillers underground', says the Scotch Whisky Association website:

A long and often bloody battle arose between the excisemen and the illicit distillers… Smuggling became standard practice for some 150 years…clandestine stills were hidden in the heather-clad hills.

In 1823 it was the Duke of Gordon, whose Speyside estate was the biggest producer, who argued for legal, licensed distilling, paving the way for industrial production. The clandestine phase meant that distilleries were often hidden at some distance from main thoroughfares, but some are close enough to railway stations to be reached on foot, including Strathisla (from Keith station), Oban, Dalwhinnie and Blair Athol (in Pitlochry).

Pretty, landscaped grounds around Strathisla, the oldest Highland distillery (established 1786). Note the 'pagodas' (technically, cupolas) topping kilns once used for malting.

Junction) met in the middle at Keith (as detailed in the section 'The Grampians: station by station', below).

Five years later, Craigellachie would gain another connection, this time heading south-west on the Strathspey line to Grantown-on-Spey: this line is described in the Lost Lines section at the end of this chapter.

Scotland's 'Lost Corner'

In his *Railway Atlas of Scotland*, David Spaven has pointed out that the coastal towns of Peterhead (population 18,500) and Fraserburgh (13,100) rank as the furthest major towns from a railway network in Britain. Only the Aberdeen–Inverness line survived the Beeching cuts, and Grampian lost many long-established railway lines and stations.

The lines opened after early parliamentary approval included, in addition to the Morayshire described above, a Morayshire Coast railway (royal assent, 1846); a line to Inverness along the Banffshire coast, rather than inland, to be built by GNOS; a separate Banff, Macduff & Turriff line and another along the coast, Banff, Portsoy & Strathisla; connections from Aberdeen through the Formantine and Buchan areas, with junctions for trains to reach Peterhead, Fraserburgh and Ellon; and a branch from Orton to Fochabers, built by Highland Railway much later, in 1893.

As a result of the twentieth-century closures – not all caused by Beeching – parts of Grampian are littered with old place names for stations or junctions that would be obscure for anyone not familiar with the railway history of the region: Strichen, Cairnbulg, Pitlurg, Auchmacoy, Udny and Philorth among them. One of these is the village of Maud, which was chosen as an important junction for trains from Aberdeen heading for Fraserburgh or Peterburgh. (Maud had another nineteenth-century feature: a large, Dickensian poorhouse.) Today, the former Maud station is a railway museum run by local volunteers.

As in other parts of the Highlands, some Grampian stations were funded privately; as Thomas

On the Moray coast, BR 78053 approaching Banff from Tillynaught (Banff, Portsoy & Strathisla line, closed in 1968).
JOHN ROBIN, 1961

and Turnock noted, 'stations were provided for the convenience of gentlemen who gave strong support'. For example, Lord Saltoun insisted on Philorth being for his own private use, so it did not feature on public timetables until after the Grouping in 1923.

The Formantine & Buchan line (1861) took the names of local Grampian areas, although the ultimate intention was to connect Aberdeen to the ports of Fraserburgh and Peterhead. From Dyce on the main line – still open today – the F&B ran through open countryside to Ellon and then to the junction at Maud. The line closed to passengers in 1965, and was then converted to a cycle and walking route taking the same name: Formantine & Buchan Way (also on the National Cycle Network). There have been discussions at regional level about reopening the Dyce–Ellon railway line.

Among other lost lines and stations was a light railway from Fraserburgh to the seaside village of St Combs, built in 1903: locomotives on the line had to be fitted with cow catchers. GNOS built a 15-mile extension from its inland junction at Ellon to the coastal resort of Boddam, mainly to service the company's Cruden Bay resort hotel and golf course.

The Grampians: Station by Station

A Historic Journey from Aberdeen to Inverness
The city of Aberdeen, where this journey starts, was profiled in the previous chapter. The descrip-

tion included the peculiar terminus, when the line started, at Kittybrewster in the north of the city, but today's journey starts from the city's only railway station, the centrally positioned Aberdeen station at the modern Union Square, fronting on to Guild Street.

Geographically, the journey must obviously head through city suburbs before reaching territory of farming and some light industry; it then leaves Aberdeenshire to cross into the council area of Moray (and the Speyside region, known for its whisky distilleries). The line then passes close to the coast of the Moray Firth before reaching the Highland Council area and its capital, Inverness. For much of the way, with some historic diversions, the line follows the path of the busy A96, the trunk road from Aberdeen to Inverness.

This line has been a focus of considerable investment (2015 onwards) by both Network Rail and ScotRail, increasing the frequency of services, double-tracking much of the former single-track line, modernising signalling and station facilities, and introducing high-speed trains (HST).

Dyce

Until 2018, passengers for Inverness had to change at Dyce, the suburban station that serves Aberdeen Airport, but the change of trains and the ten-minute wait have been eliminated, taking nearly half an hour off the original journey time, bringing it down to around two and a quarter hours.

Dyce was involved in early railway development in the region, but the town has since been absorbed into the Aberdeen conurbation and is best known as the site of the city's airport. Passenger numbers through Dyce have quadrupled since the turn of the century. A Dyce station opened on the first line (GNOS, 1854) between Aberdeen (Kittybrewster) and Huntly, and it became a junction in 1858 with the opening of the Formantine & Buchan line, subsequently closed.

Kintore

Ten miles up the line, Kintore is another expanding destination, described by NESTRANS as 'the fastest growing town in Aberdeenshire'. Its former station (1854–1964) was scheduled to reopen in 2020 with modern practical features but also with an ultra-modern attention to the environment (bio-diverse landscaping), and opportunities for local artists to display their work.

Inverurie

Inverurie (with a population of 13,640) was an agri-

Inverurie Works (1902–1969) developed by GNOS. The Vaughan crane could lift 125 tons.
SRPS

Insch's Station Hotel, reopened in 2019, offering 'craft beer, Sky Sports, fresh coffee, live music'… The station itself, across the street, contains the Insch Connection Museum.

cultural market town that is increasingly home to Aberdeen commuters. In local rail history, Inverurie is remembered for its locomotive repair centre, operating from 1902 to 1969; its Highland League football team honours the memory as Inverurie Loco Works FC. Yet another long-lost line ran from Inverurie (then 'Inverury') from 1856 to 1966, covering the 8 miles north-east to Oldmeldrum.

Just beyond Inverurie is a reminder of Scotland's turbulent past: the railway line skirts a field at Harlaw where a famous clan battle in 1411 resulted in some 1,500 deaths. Today, near the site of the battle, the railway line is bridged by the A96, the trunk road that parallels the railway for most of the way to Inverness. Cars and trains hurtle past the formerly isolated station of Inveramsay, yet another old junction station (closed 1951) on this line. Here, passengers changed from the GNOS on to the Banff, Macduff & Turriff Junction, or vice versa.

Insch

Next stop is Insch (population 2,282), set in pleasant, rolling countryside – although an Aberdeen estate agent has described the village as 'an ideal spot for commuters', with its regular and faster rail service. The village offers a primary school and nursery, a health centre and easy access to hill walks or golf. The station has its own small museum – Insch Connection – which illustrates village history and includes a model of the railway station 'in the days when the layout of tracks was complex'. Opposite is the elegant Station Hotel, which reopened in 2019 after lying empty for eight years.

Huntly

Having forked away from the A96 near Insch, the railway heads into open countryside, following the line of the B9002 and the River Bogie, and then curving north to reach Huntly (population 8,000), just short of an hour from Aberdeen. This was the original Great North terminus: on 19 September 1854, a set of twenty-five carriages arrived for the grand opening of Aberdeen–Huntly, carrying 650 people for a special celebration on the platform. About 400 had started in Aberdeen, the remainder joining at nine stations: of these, Buxsburn, Pitcaple, Oyne, Kennethmont and Gartly were eventually closed down.

Keith

Two years after Huntly's grand opening, the GNOS line was extended across the county boundary from Aberdeenshire to Morayshire (once called Elginshire, now just Moray) to arrive at Keith (population 4,750). The town holds a memorable role because the GNOS line from Aberdeen met the Inverness & Aberdeen Junction here, although another two years went by before connection in August 1858.

Keith was also a terminus for the Moray Coast Line and was therefore known formerly as Keith Junction. (Keith Town station was built separately for Keith & Dufftown: *see* the section 'Lost Lines and Heritage in Grampian' at the end of this chapter.) Today, Keith is noted as being home to the Strathisla whisky distillery, named after the broad valley or 'strath' of the River Isla that flows into the River Deveron as a tributary and eventually

into the Moray Firth at Banff. Built in 1786, Strathisla claims to be the oldest operating distillery in Scotland.

Whisky comes to the fore when the train leaves Keith, the line running alongside a chain of thirty warehouses for storing whisky in casks; as the Strathisla distillery, the whisky here is owned by Chivas Regal, part of the French drinks multinational, Pernod Ricard. The train also passes close to the Auchroisk distillery, which, in contrast to Strathisla, only dates back to the 1970s.

Just after Auchroisk, the train crosses the River Spey and then picks up speed through former stations at Orton – originally a junction on Morayshire Railway; at Orbliston – a junction for the Fochabers branch (Highland Railway, 1893); and at Lhanbryde.

Elgin

Elgin (population 23,130), the capital of the Moray region, already had a station by 1852 on the short line to Lossiemouth (Morayshire Railway, later GNOS). It was renamed later as Elgin East, when Inverness & Aberdeen arrived from the west, opening their own station as Elgin West; the stations were a third of a mile apart, but both were situated on the southern edge of the town centre. The Elgin West site was used for the merged stations (March 1858), modernized in 1990; the East station closed with the

Former Elgin East station (under Morayshire, then GNOS). It was closed in 1968, and converted to offices. SRPS

end of the line to Craigellachie under Beeching in 1968.

A ten-minute walk takes passengers to Elgin High Street, or a fifteen-minute walk takes visitors to the ruins of Elgin Cathedral. Built in 1224, the cathedral suffered violent damage in subsequent centuries: it was fired in 1390 by the Earl of Buchan (or the 'Wolf of Badenoch'), and finally closed by the Reformation in 1560.

A further five minutes on foot takes the visitor to Johnstons of Elgin, one of the last woollen mills in Scotland, dating back to 1797. Specializing in cashmere, the factory with its shops and a restaurant make Johnstons a popular visitor attraction.

Forres, one of Scotland's recently rebuilt stations (2017): functional if bland, with lifts and a sheltered walkway between platforms.

Forres

Back on the train, a twelve-minute run from Elgin reaches Forres (population 12,500), a prosperous and pretty town and a regular winner in the Britain in Bloom awards. As at Elgin, there is a ten-minute walk to the High Street.

In contrast to other stations on this line, Forres station is completely modern, having been rebuilt in 2017 with state-of-the-art features such as a 160m platform for future five-coach HSTs to use, new ticket machines and customer information screens (CIS), and a large car park. (The original nineteenth-century station had itself been modernized in the mid-1950s.) The latest reconstruction was carried out as part of the £170 million programme of improvements on the Aberdeen–Inverness line.

The Forres area was involved in two earlier railway lines – *see* the section 'Lost Lines and Heritage in Grampian' later in this chapter – of which the most important was the southbound connection to Grantown-on-Spey. To the north, a short line was built from Kinloss to the coast at Findhorn in 1860. Kinloss was an RAF base from 1939 to 2011 (it is

retained as barracks), while Lossiemouth, further along the Moray coast, is still active as a base for fighter aircraft. Findhorn, in contrast, is home to Findhorn Foundation, a New Age community.

Nairn

From Forres, the line reaches the coast at Nairn (population 9,775), which was the original terminus for trains out of Inverness (Inverness & Nairn, authorized in 1854, later absorbed by Inverness & Aberdeen Junction and then by Highland Railway). The original station opened to great fanfare on 5 November 1855, the maiden journey involving some 800 passengers, mostly on open wagons, as recorded by the Inverness Courier:

> Almost all the way they sang songs in loud chorus, and testified by the exhilaration of spirits that they were not unacquainted with the barley-bree [whisky] of Nairnshire. There was, however, no excess.

Thanks to its railway and to its extensive sandy beaches, Nairn developed as an important seaside resort – the actor Charlie Chaplin spent many summers here – and it retains good hotels, caravan sites and championship golf courses. The enlarged second station, built in 1885, preserves a 'particularly rich and complete representation of a late nineteenth-century Highland Railway station' (according to Historic Environment Scotland, the government agency). Unusually it had two signal boxes, one at each end of the passing loop; because of the distance between them a bicycle was provided for the signalman to ride from one to the other.

Into Inverness

From Nairn, the final stretch into Inverness is less picturesque than the run through Speyside or the other routes out of Inverness, but prosperity is evident, as is the inexorable spreading outward of the Highland capital. There is rich farmland here – grain and livestock – and some light industry before the railway line skirts Inverness airport. There have been plans to open a new station to serve the airport, an industrial estate and the new town of Tornagrain, but with no date fixed for the opening. The proposed site would be close to Dalcross, where a station closed in 1965 after exactly one hundred years in operation.

'Lost Stations'

Finally, in this station-by-station section, three interesting 'lost stations' should be mentioned. They originally lined up between Nairn and Inverness:

Cawdor: Later renamed Kildrummie Junction, Cawdor principally served Cawdor Castle (dating from the fifteenth century) and its aristocratic inhabitants, the Earl and Countess of Cawdor. (Shakespeare describes Macbeth – without historic basis – as the Thane of Cawdor.)

Fort George station: This station was renamed Gollanfield Junction, though it also served the village of Ardersier, taking the name of the awe-inspiring military fort that overlooks the Moray Firth. Still used by the British Army as a garrison and training camp – although open to public visits – the fort was built in the late 1700s, named after King George II, to guard against another Jacobite rebellion in the Highlands.

Culloden: Later called Allanfearn, Culloden is a village a short drive from the battlefield of Culloden Moor, where the Jacobite Rebellion of 1745–46 culminated in defeat for Bonnie Prince Charlie.

Rural old Dalcross station (1865–1965) from the west. A new Dalcross station is under planning in 2020. SRPS

The Culloden battlefield and famous viaduct are described in the next chapter.

Lost Lines and Heritage in Grampian

At the start of this chapter, in the section 'Scotland's Lost Corner', the presence of many closed lines in the Grampian region was noted (Morayshire, Moray Coast and other coastal lines, such as Banff, Portsoy & Strathisla: in the first episode of 'Walking Britain's Lost Railways' – Channel 5, 2018 – presenter Rob Bell walked the remains of the lines from Elgin to Lossiemouth and Portsoy to Cullen, where parts of the viaducts survive).

Then there was the Formantine & Buchan, which connected the large seaside ports of Fraserburgh and Peterhead, also serving Maud and Ellon. Taking a broader view of the region, these were in addition to the Royal Deeside, documented in the previous chapter.

Several other equally significant lines ran through Grampian, much to the west of those already mentioned and making connections to the Main Line (*see* Chapter 4), but their origins in the Grampian region make them worthy of presenting here.

Keith & Dufftown

The Keith & Dufftown Railway Association was set up in 1998 – exactly thirty years after the original GNOS line closed – and since 2000 has offered summer services for groups of ten or more, mostly on Class 108 DMUs. The terminus station at Dufftown has a restored booking office and waiting room, and catering from a carriage café facing the platform. The line was preserved for specials between official closure in 1968 and 1991.

ScotRail's modern Keith station was originally a junction serving separately owned lines out of Aberdeen and Inverness; it is situated a fifteen-minute walk from the town centre, whereas the old Keith Town station now serves as a terminus and HQ for the heritage line, Keith & Dufftown. The line runs for 11 miles along Glen Isla to the centre of Duff-

Sign at the entrance to the heritage line for Keith & Dufftown, the 'Whisky Line'. The badge shows it is a four-star visitor attraction ('Scottish Tourist Board', now VisitScotland).

town, which, despite its small population (1,700), claims to be the 'whisky capital of the world', being surrounded by many famous distilleries including Glenfiddich – the world's number one single malt brand – and Balvenie. The original line turned north from Dufftown to run past even more distilleries – Macallan, Aberlour, Glen Grant – on its route via Craigellachie and Rothes to Elgin.

Grantown-on-Spey

Until the Beeching era closures, Grantown-on-Spey had occupied an important position in Grampian railways, with two lines meeting there. The town (population 2,500) was created by the local Grant family – landowners and whisky distillers – in 1766. The arrival of railways in 1863 boosted the town both agriculturally and industrially, but their main effect was to promote Victorian tourism to the area, as evidenced even today by the large number of hotels and guest houses.

In the same year, 1863, two lines (and stations) arrived in 'Grantown': the GNOS-owned line from the east (originally the independent Strathspey Railway, as it is known today for heritage purposes) and a line from the north – the Inverness & Perth Junction, which met the established Aberdeen–Inverness line at Forres, near the Moray Firth. A triangu-

Aberlour, a former stop on the Strathspey Line, survives as the home of Speyside Way visitor centre. The old platform looks out on to a pleasant riverside park.

lar junction was created near Forres to facilitate the crossing of the lines.

Because the line from Forres to Grantown was built as part of the original 'main line' serving Inverness from the south, its details will be given in the next chapter, covering the development of today's Main Line.

The Strathspey, meanwhile, had independently connected Dufftown with Grantown in 1863, but within three years it was part of Great North of Scotland. Dufftown had connections to Elgin and Keith on the main Aberdeen–Inverness route, but the primary function of the Strathspey was to serve distilleries in the area. From Dufftown the line offered fourteen stops before Grantown, including names associated with whisky such as Craigellachie, Aberlour, Knockando and Ballindalloch.

Unfortunately for the town of Grantown-on-Spey, neither railway company saw fit to invest in a joint station in 1863, so Grantown West (as it become known) served the line from Forres (absorbed eventually by Highland Railway), while GNOS/Strathspey trains pulled in to Grantown East, both stations a fairly considerable hike from the town centre. Grantown West station was entirely demolished; at the site of Grantown East station, a heritage company created a Highland Heritage & Cultural Centre in 2018, with a converted restaurant car and a miniature steam railway.

There is further coverage of the lines from Grantown-on-Spey in the next chapter, about the Main Line.

Services on the Aberdeen–Inverness Line

In 2019 (19 August–14 December), ScotRail operated the following Aberdeen–Inverness services:

- Aberdeen–Inverness: Mon.–Sat.: Eleven daily, all stops as described above. Sun.: Five daily, starting from 10.00 (last train 21.27)

- Aberdeen to Inverurie only: Eleven daily, also two daily to Dyce only
- Inverness–Aberdeen: Mon.–Sat.: Eleven daily, all stops, of which one through to Edinburgh (dep. Inverness 4.53)

Sources for Grampian Railways

(*See* also the Sources chapter for general sources.)

The History of the Railways of the Scottish Highlands (series 1977–1990):
   Originally published by David & Charles, now from House of Lochar, Isle of Colonsay
   3. Vallance, H.A., *The Great North of Scotland Railway*

Great North of Scotland Railway Association (publisher)
   Fenwick, K., Flett, D. and Jackson, D., *Railways of Buchan* (2008)
   Jackson, D., *Rails to Alford: Story of the Railway from Kintore to Alford* (2006)
   Jackson, D., *Royal Deeside's Railway: Aberdeen to Ballater* (1999)
   Jones, K. G., *The Railways of Aberdeen: 150 Years of History* (2000)

Burgess, R. and Kinghorn, R., *Moray Coast Railways* (Mercat Press 1989)
Stansfield, G., *Banff, Moray and Nairn's Lost Railways* (Stenlake 2000)

Thomas, J. and Turnock, D., *A Regional History of the Railways of Great Britain Vol 15: The North of Scotland* (David & Charles 1989)

Internet (www.)
Great North of Scotland Railway Association
(gnsra.org.uk)

Keith & Dufftown Railway
(keith-dufftown-railway.co.uk)

NESTRANS: North East Scotland Transport Partnership
(nestrans.org.uk)

Network Rail
(networkrail.co.uk) – page on Aberdeen–Inverness

Railscot.co.uk – primary resource for Scottish railway information

ScotRail
(ScotRail.co.uk) – official website of Abellio franchise

scot-rail
(scot-rail.co.uk) – 'Scotland's online rail enthusiast community'

CHAPTER 4

Scotland's Backbone: the Highland Main Line

If the map of Scotland is visualized as a human body, its waist would be the Central Belt from Edinburgh to Glasgow, then the Highlands form the torso, the arms extending down the coasts east and west, and the Highland Main Line would be the 'backbone', which runs up through the centre from south to north.

The route northwards from Perth to Inverness is described by both ScotRail and Network Rail as the Main Line (ScotRail is the passenger service for rail travel in Scotland, while Network Rail is the UK agency for the railway infrastructure); this differentiates it from two other long-distance routes into the Highlands: up the east coast, through Fife and Angus, and up the west coast to Fort William (through Argyll & Bute into Highland region).

This chapter describes the central route northwards via Perth and Aviemore, but the journey is

Class 170 (170396) southbound negotiating the viaduct at Slochd, a high point on the Highland Main. Grey rock infill dates back to a landslip in 2012.

given context by including a departure from Glasgow. (There are also direct trains from Edinburgh to Inverness; both routes pass through Perth.)

Genesis of the Main Line

Today, the Main Line warrants its name, as it is the busiest rail route from the Central Belt into the Highlands – but this was not always the case. The earliest non-stop, long-distance rail journeys into the Highlands took place on the east coast, as explained in Chapter 2. There were several reasons for this, including the location on the east coast of Edinburgh, Dundee and Aberdeen, and the impetus provided by Queen Victoria's visits to Balmoral, her Highland home. But basic geography also played its part: it was much easier to lay tracks on the flat lands of Fife, Angus and Aberdeenshire than through the hills and mountains of Scotland's central 'backbone' region.

The challenge of climbing into the Cairngorms and crossing mountain passes at Drumochter and Slochd will be described in this chapter. The map of physical geography shows that to travel directly north from Glasgow is to immediately encounter the hilly, semi-rural areas of the Campsie Fells and the Trossachs (a scenic area marketed as 'the Highlands in miniature' and preserved as part of Loch Lomond and The Trossachs National Park; the terrain includes a small range of hills crossed by the Duke's Pass and several lochs).

The west was even more challenging; its railway finally opened in 1901, decades later than those of other Scottish regions.

The original idea, therefore, was to take the east coast route to Aberdeen and change there, crossing Grampian to reach Inverness (a route completed by 1858). An alternative, developed in the 1860s, was to change trains at Forres (on the Aberdeen–Inverness line) and head south on the rural line via Grantown-on-Spey, then westwards to meet a line coming up the centre from Perth and Dunkeld. It was also possible, circuitously, to travel from Aberdeen on Great North of Scotland lines through whisky country (Dufftown, Craigellachie and so on) to reach Grantown-on-Spey.

The 'direct' route north was not even given parliamentary approval until the 1880s, and this line would not reach Inverness until 1898.

Peaks and Passes: The Engineering Challenge

The land abounded in long, steep gradients and spectacular summits ...tunnels were eschewed in the hill regions of Scotland, which meant that the engineers took their lines over mountain passes.

The Scottish Railway Book (John Thomas, 1977)

As pointed out by the prolific author Oswald Nock (1905–94), who wrote twenty-eight railway books including *Scottish Railways* (1950) and *The Railway Enthusiast's Encyclopedia* (1968), there were challenging climbs on all Highland lines except the east coast. For example, the ascent from Inverness to reach Aviemore had 'an extremely severe start for southbound trains in steam days; double-heading was commonplace'. Having to pause halfway along these stretches was also awkward for steam-powered locomotives.

Although summits could be bypassed and tunnels were usually deemed unnecessary, the Highland locomotives nevertheless faced the challenge of long inclines, sometimes at harsh gradients, to reach the summits. Nock identified the following climbs as the most onerous in the Highlands:

- On the West Highland, Fort William–Corrour: 28 miles, average gradient 1:110 but 1:67 on the 10-mile stretch from Tulloch–Corrour. Also Ardlui–Crianlarich, 16 miles at 1:60–1:70
- On the Highland Main, Inverness–Slochd (22 miles between 1:60 and 1:90) and Blair Atholl–Drumochter (17 miles, 1:70–1:85)
- Two difficult stretches on lines now closed were from Forres to Dava (Forres–Aviemore), 15 miles at 1:75, and through Glen Ogle (Callander–Oban), 6 miles at 1:60

The very highest Scottish rail summits are in the Borders at Wanlockhead (1,498ft) (the Leadhills &

Wanlockhead branch, built to serve a lead-mining area, closed in 1939; a heritage group, Lowthers Railway Society, is rebuilding narrow-gauge track on the old way), followed by Drumochter (1,484ft) and Slochd (1,315ft) on the Highland Main. Their heights above sea level are modest enough by global standards, but they provide good views, which can be bleak or beautiful, depending on the mountain weather conditions.

The other Highland summits over 1,000ft are both on the West Highland Line at the crossroads town of Tyndrum (1,024ft, at Upper Tyndrum station), and further north in the Rannoch Moor wilderness at remote Corrour station (1,350ft).

Why so few Tunnels in the Highlands?

In spite of its mountainous character, Scotland has few notable tunnels ... engineers were more concerned with burrowing under urban areas than boring through mountains.

The Scottish Railway Book (John Thomas, 1977)

As mentioned by Oswald Nock in the earlier quote ('tunnels were eschewed'), the Scottish Highlands feature very few tunnels of any great length, in contrast to railways in other mountainous parts of Europe. On the original Highland Railway and Great North of Scotland routes, only seven tunnels were created with a total length of less than one mile.

In a landscape that is hilly but smoothed over by the Ice Age and constant weathering, engineers found it relatively easy to pass around or over the hills, and with such a low population density, there was less need for the effort and cost of tunnelling that applies in the busy Alps, for example. There were some exceptions in building the extension from Fort William to Mallaig, where undulating coastal land, interspersed with burns and rivers, necessitated a number of relatively short tunnels, bridges and viaducts.

Tunnels were sometimes incorporated because landowners insisted that railway lines should not spoil the views from their stately homes. The 600-yard Kippenross tunnel, near Dunblane, is the second longest (after Moncrieffe) outside Glasgow and Edinburgh; the Railscot website dismisses it as 'an unnecessary tunnel forced on the railway by the landowner, who did not wish a railway line to cross their property'.

Anderston Cross (2,800 yards) and London Road (1,300yd) in Glasgow, and Waverley–Haymarket

There are few tunnels in the Highlands generally, but there are seven like this near Lochailort on the Fort William–Mallaig line. SRPS

(1,009yd) in Edinburgh, are among the urban tunnels with heavy use. The world's four longest rail tunnels are all over 30 miles long: Gotthard Base in Switzerland; Seikan in Japan; Eurotunnel, France/UK; and Yulhyeon in Korea.

The Highland Main Line: Station by Station

A Historic Journey from Glasgow to Inverness

A characteristic of the long journey northwards up the 'backbone' is a passage through some quite desolate wilderness areas, high above sea level, before the line descends gracefully into the Highland capital. Along the way, the Main Line passes through gentle, rural Perth and Kinross into the Highland Council area; with all possible stops made, only eleven stations are visited over a distance of 170 miles, so the stops are few and far between compared to other Scottish railway routes.

The Main Line mostly follows the same path as a busy trunk road, the A9, the long route north from Edinburgh, which is a motorway as far as Stirling and then drops down to A-road status, some of it dual carriageway.

Queen Street

The starting point for this journey is Glasgow's Queen Street station, rebuilt between 2017 and 2020, having originated as the terminus of the Edinburgh & Glasgow Line in 1842. At that time, Glasgow's population was rocketing (from 77,000 in 1801 to 275,000 in 1841) as industry and shipbuilding combined to make it the Second City of Empire, but with the attendant problems of overcrowding. Industrial decline in the twentieth century reduced the city's population from 1.5 million to 600,000, but decades of depression have been overcome by investment in business, culture and sport.

Central and Queen Street are the two main Glasgow stations, both starting points for long-distance train journeys. Built on two levels, Queen Street's street-level platforms serve Edinburgh and the north, while the low level serves the suburban North Clyde Line and also the West Highland Line (and the Caledonian Sleeper).

From Glasgow Queen Street, the line runs north-eastwards through the densely populated Central Belt – towns including Larbert and Falkirk – but then swerves north to enter the flood plain of the River Forth. This Main Line train is bound for the Highlands and is not intended to serve the Central Belt, so it is a twenty-seven-minute, non-stop phase of the journey from Glasgow to Stirling.

Stirling

Stirling (with a population of 36,000) is famous for its castle and the medieval battles fought here, which

Stirling Castle standing above flat 'carse' land, marking the division between the Lowlands and the Highlands.

defined Scotland's independence from English control. The Battle of Stirling Bridge (1297) was made famous by Mel Gibson's *Braveheart* (1997), portraying national hero William Wallace. The Battle of Bannockburn (1314) was a Scottish victory under King Robert the Bruce. The reigning Stuart family favoured Stirling Castle as a residence for over two centuries.

Trains from Stirling depart frequently for Glasgow, Edinburgh, Inverness, Dundee and Aberdeen – a fitting place in the rail network for a city that prides itself as the Brooch of Scotland, linking the main cities of the Highlands and Lowlands.

Dunblane

Just north of Stirling comes a stop at Dunblane, which offers rail connections to both Glasgow and Edinburgh and is therefore a popular town of residence for commuters to either city. At one time Dunblane was the starting point of a complicated but useful route across Scotland to the western port of Oban, on a line now seen as one of the country's most regretted lost lines.

Gleneagles

As the commuter belt thins out after Dunblane, the train usually speeds through Gleneagles station – served only four times daily – which opened in 1919 for the nearby Gleneagles Hotel and golf resort. Until rationalization of the old Scottish Central lines there were seven other small stations on this route. Most unusual was Carsebreck, a private

station for the Royal Caledonian Curling Club; the nearby pond regularly froze over in winter, enabling the bonspiel (curling tournaments) to be held here.

The Dunblane–Perth leg, like Glasgow–Stirling, is a lengthy one, taking twenty-six minutes if there is no stop at Gleneagles. Just outside Perth, this Glasgow line meets the Edinburgh line at Hilton Junction, and then the trains enter Moncrieffe Tunnel, the longest railway tunnel in the Highlands, burrowing for just 1,220 yards under Friarton Quarry and a modern road junction (M90, A90, A912).

Perth

Perth (population 47,000) is reached exactly one hour after departing Queen Street on the 7.10. Many would consider this city to be the starting point of the Highland Line.

> It was inevitable that Perth would become the major railway junction in the north of Scotland, with six main lines converging on the city by the end of the century, not to mention the cross-country route to Crieff, Balquhidder and Oban.
>
> North of Scotland (John Thomas and David Turnock 1989)

Known as the 'Fair City', Perth developed at the lowest bridging point of the River Tay, Scotland's longest river (117 miles). For over 500 years, Scottish kings were anointed at Scone, next to Perth, while seated on the Stone of Destiny (now kept at Edinburgh Castle).

All Aboard! Perth Station

The importance of Perth station, originally built in 1847, is reflected in its impressive scale and features: seven long platforms, an ample car park, and the

Platform 7 at Perth: the station identifier is in the modern ScotRail blue/white, but the older brown/cream scheme (BR) has been preserved.

A 'railbus' at Crieff (1856–1964) on the 7-mile Crieff–Comrie branch (1856–1964). Detailed at https://www.railcar.co.uk/data/vehicle/79969. SRPS

adjacent Station Hotel. Architecturally listed since 1977, the back section of the station retains some original BR livery of brown and cream.

In the heady days of railway 'mania' – the 1840s and 1850s – Perth found itself being served by several companies with interlocking interests (later to amalgamate): Scottish Central, Dundee & Perth, Edinburgh & Northern (for Fife), Scottish Midland Junction (to Forfar), Perth & Dunkeld, Caledonian and North British. Today, there are ScotRail long-distance services to both Glasgow and Edinburgh from Inverness and regular departures to Dundee, following the line of the River Tay.

The hotel opened in 1890; Queen Victoria was a regular guest, so a royal passage was built from the station into the hotel. The current owners have retained the 'grand rooms, sweeping staircases and high ceilings', features that survive in many of the large hotels built to serve nineteenth-century city stations (for example the Royal Highland at Inverness and the Aberdeen Station hotel).

Lines to and from Perth

Perth was connected early on (1847) to Dundee, eastwards alongside the River Tay, and separately (by Scottish Midland Junction, 1848) to Forfar, with the eventual aim of reaching the North Sea coast and Aberdeen. Meanwhile, Perth was linked south-westwards to Stirling in the same year (1848) under Scottish Central, this line connecting to Edinburgh & Glasgow and forming a basis of the present Main Line. Ten years later (1858), a route westwards was achieved, but this time linking much smaller communities on the Perth, Almond Valley & Meth-

ven and an extension to Crieff. By the mid-1860s, amalgamation had consigned the names of all these central Scotland lines to the history books, while the towns they connected were mostly cast adrift in the twentieth century (*see* Lost Lines, later in this chapter).

Yet another railway aiming at Perth came up from Edinburgh through Fife (from the south-east) with stations at Ladybank and Bridge of Earn, which are important today; originally called Edinburgh & Northern, the line passed to the larger North British in 1862. This was long before the Forth Bridge (1890) was built, so ferries served the line over the river at Burntisland; passengers had to change trains on either side of the Forth, but an early 'roll-on, roll-off' system was used so that wagons could be ramped on to the ferries, rather than transferring the freight by hand.

For the Highlands, the most lasting legacy of mid-nineteenth-century building was the direct northward line, Perth & Dunkeld (1856), which became part of today's Main Line. However, that modest 15-mile stretch would encapsulate Scottish (and British) railway history by having a dozen owners or operators in its history to date: independent from 1854 to 1856, then operated by Scottish Midland Junction and Scottish North Eastern; absorbed by Inverness & Perth Junction in 1864, then part of Highland Railway from 1865; and eventually subsumed under London Midland & Scottish (LMS), British Rail (Scottish Region) and ScotRail.

The line from Perth to Dunkeld takes a historic diversion away from the logical line northwards, followed by the A9 trunk road (and old military roads). After Luncarty (the station closed in 1951), there is an eastward loop around the former stations at Stanley and Stanley Junction, which served the old Scottish Midland Junction on its way to Forfar (and Aberdeen).

Just south of Dunkeld, the line crosses the Highland Boundary Fault, taking the train officially into the Highland zone, as geologically defined.

Dunkeld & Birnam

The station at Dunkeld & Birnam was originally Birnam & Dunkeld (1856–61), then Dunkeld (to 1903), Dunkeld & Birnam to 1981, then had another spell as just Dunkeld to 1991, and is now back to Dunkeld & Birnam! This duality recognized the significance of the two separate, but adjacent, villages: Dunkeld, famous for its medieval cathedral and peaceful setting on the River Tay, and Birnam, mentioned by Shakespeare ('Macbeth shall never vanquished be until Great Birnam Wood to high Dunsinane Hill shall come against him'), and later associated with Beatrix Potter, the English children's author, who spent childhood holidays here.

Dunkeld & Birnam station has several interesting features:

- Not uncommonly among Highland stations is the station's distance from the town centre (or rather, centres): a 300-yard path to Birnam and a mile on foot to Dunkeld. The route of the A9 runs between station and town and is due to be 'dualled', with a further possible impact on the station
- The low platforms necessitate portable yellow steps (shown in the photograph), and ScotRail warns passengers that using the station is unsuitable for those with impaired mobility: 'If heading north, passengers will need to be assisted off the train at Perth and taxied to Dunkeld or Pitlochry if heading south' (the station at Dunkeld & Birnam being unstaffed)
- There is a handsome, listed station building (closed to the public), and the footbridge and signal box (1919) are also listed. Dunkeld & Birnam was the last station in Scotland to exchange gas lighting for electricity, as late as 1980

From Dunkeld & Birnam station, the train follows a fairly straight path for several miles alongside the Tay, where anglers can often be seen wading, hoping to catch salmon or trout. Along this line there were stations at Dalguise (to 1965), Guay (1959) and

Dunkeld & Birnam's low platforms with steps to assist passengers in boarding modern trains (a feature at several Highland stations).

Pitlochry 'up' platform (southbound); the station buildings are in stone, with a waiting area under the awning, toilets and a bookshop.

Ballinluig (1965), which was the start of the 10-mile branch line to Aberfeldy (to 1965).

Pitlochry

The town of Pitlochry (population 2,775) has not always been acknowledged enough in Scottish railway histories. Although it was never likely to become a junction for other railways, Pitlochry is a natural 'pause' for travellers through this part of Scotland, separated as it is by at least 25 miles in all directions from the nearest towns or cities:

> From Perth to Pitlochry is a railway journey not to be excelled if equalled in Scotland for variety and beauty of scenery. The traveller will probably pay a visit to beautiful Dunkeld, but will do well to stop a few days at Pitlochry. We put up for the night at the splendid hotel owned by Mr Fisher, capable of entertaining 150 guests and which in summer is crowded to overflowing.

> *Whisky Distilleries of the United Kingdom* (1887) by Alfred Barnard, quoted in *North of Scotland* (Thomas, J. and Turnock, D.)

Aided by the railway reaching it in 1863 on the Inverness & Perth Junction Line, Pitlochry rose to prominence as a Victorian Highland retreat. Massive hotels such as Fishers, Atholl Palace and the 'Hydro' developed, and the twentieth century brought new attractions for tourists: two distilleries open to visitors (Blair Athol and Edradour); the Festival Theatre, capable of staging 'West End' productions; and the Fish Ladder, a series of pools on the River Tummel where salmon can be seen leaping.

All Aboard! Pitlochry Station

Pitlochry's station sits conveniently on a quiet side street off the main road through town next to the bus terminus, coach park and public toilets.

Established in 1863 by Inverness & Perth Junction (absorbed by Highland Railway in 1865), the station buildings were later rebuilt with distinctly different structures on either platform.

The Scottish Tudor-style building on the up (southbound) platform is in natural stone with crowstep gables over an awning-protected waiting area. The northbound (down) platform building has a pretty mixture of blue-painted timber, slate roof, red-brick chimneys and a decorative roof-ridge in terracotta.

Today, the station is proudly looked after by the local Community Railway Partnership (CRP) for the Highland Main Line. It is one of 275 ScotRail stations involved in partnerships. Since its adoption, Pitlochry has had a bookshop for second-hand books – offering a free Heritage Trail map of the town – together with a display of old photographs of the station, a restored 1911 drinking fountain, a mural and posters by local schoolchildren and, as usual on adopted stations, colourful displays of hanging baskets and 'barrel-train' planters.

Blair Atholl

On leaving Pitlochry northbound, there is a relatively short run – for the Highland Line – of just nine minutes to Blair Atholl, serving the village of that name. The village is home to only around 500 people, but the station owes its location to being on the Atholl estate, serving nearby Blair Castle, the most important tourist attraction in this area. The seat of the dukes of Atholl, the castle is at the centre of a 143,700-acre estate with agriculture, forestry and housing operations and a heavy investment in tourism: camping, tractor tours, pony trekking, grouse shooting, and special events such as an annual international horse trials competition.

Blair Atholl station is one of many across the Highlands whose existence was influenced by local landowners, particularly the nobility. Queen Victoria used the station, en route to Balmoral, on a visit to the Duke of Atholl a week after it opened in September 1963.

An eccentric fact about Blair Atholl is that the water supply for the village was once managed by railway companies, which needed to ensure a supply for their steam locomotives. Network Rail finally handed over the supply to the national agency, Scottish Water, in 2006.

Leaving Blair Atholl

After Blair Atholl there is a long (25-minute) run through the sparsely populated Glen Garry and the Pass of Drumochter (also spelled Druimuachdar),

Blair Castle: uniquely among Scottish castles, it is painted white; the core building is a medieval tower house (1269), extended and remodelled in the seventeenth and nineteenth centuries.
ISTOCK.COM/STANFAIR

HIGHLAND RAILWAYS AND THE GREAT LANDOWNERS

Scotland's aristocracy was based largely on the traditional clan system, with clan chiefs being granted titles and privileges within Scotland and later within the United Kingdom. These chiefdoms and titles invariably came with ownership of large estates, many of which were peaking in size in the nineteenth century when railways were being built.

Most notable of these aristocratic landowners, in the railway context, were the dukes of Sutherland, of Atholl and of Argyll. The Duke of Sutherland, who sponsored the building of railways in Caithness (*see* Chapter 5, the Far North Line), owned the largest estate in Europe in the mid-nineteenth century, at 1.3 million acres (although it is much reduced since that time). The Atholl estate once occupied 200,000 acres of Perthshire (143,700 today), while the Argyll estate (the Campbell clan chief), in the west, once comprised 175,000 acres.

Landlords could, and did, either block or divert railways through their estates, but some (such as the Duke of Sutherland) also contributed as developers, whether financially or in their role as Members of Parliament. Modern ScotRail lines run through various Highland estates owned by wealthy individuals or by organizations such as The National Trust for Scotland.

the absence of stations combined with the mountain gradients helping to explain why the full Highland Main Line was completed so late (1890s). As Thomas and Turnock put it in *North of Scotland*, the railway when first proposed in the 1840s would be '120 miles long through desolate country with no towns, no coal, no industry and very few people'.

Note that another, more famous river, River (and Glen) Garry, feeds into Loch Oich, in the Great Glen, at the town of Invergarry, which once gave its name to the ill-fated Invergarry & Fort Augustus railway company. (Neither glen is connected to the stage play entitled Glengarry Glen Ross [David Mamet, 1984].)

Despite the relative desolation, there were minor stations and halts along this line – up to Beeching in the mid-1960s – including Black Island Platform, passed just after Blair Atholl, a private halt for a logging camp, and Struan and Dalnaspidal. The latter once held the record as Britain's highest station on a principal railway line, at 1,405ft. Dalnaspidal's timber station building was

dismantled and taken to Aviemore for use by the Strathspey heritage railway, and was later moved to the grounds of Inshriach House near Aviemore.

To reach Drumochter Summit, there is a gradient to climb of 1:85 for nearly 5 miles, and this inhibited early plans for a railway here, whilst also stimulating engineers and designers to come up with solutions. Among them were David Jones, Locomotive Superintendent of Highland Railway from 1870 to 1896, who introduced the first locomotive with a wheel arrangement of 4-6-0 on a British railway

View from the A9 road to Loch Garry at the start of Drumochter Pass. The rosebay-willowherb (pink) is in full flower, and ragwort (yellow) in the foreground; note the old military road, now a trail.

line to help with heavy freight loads in the High-lands. The first of the 'Jones Goods' class, Highland Railway 103, built in 1894, can be seen at Glasgow's Riverside Museum of Transport. Snowploughs had to be fitted to the noses of locomotives working the Highland Main in winter.

Once Drumochter Pass is negotiated, the peaks of Glas Mheall Mor (3,212ft) and Carn Na Caim (3,087ft) tower over the railway to the north and west, marking the beginning of the Cairngorms National Park, the Grampian region and the High-land council area. The railway line comes close to the A9, where a snow gate provides evidence that winter conditions can be severe enough to close the road. On a clear day, however, a magnificent view emerges of Loch Ericht, stretching 15 miles long (but only a half-mile wide) to the south-west. There

are hydro-electric stations and dams at both ends of the loch.

Dalwhinnie

Trains from Drumochter descend into the village of Dalwhinnie, situated where the northern dam of Loch Ericht meets the start of Glen Truim, a long and broad valley heading northwards, along which rail and road will travel. Meaning 'meeting place' in Gaelic, Dalwhinnie is famous for its whisky distillery, which once had its own siding. Owned by Diageo and popular for giving tours, the distillery is renowned for its white-painted exterior and 'pago-das', which are seen prominently by drivers on the A9. (Railway passengers miss this view, as the line passes the back of the distillery.)

After Dalwhinnie, the line enters the broadening valley of Glen Truim, with the A9 on the right and an unmarked road running parallel on the left. This is a modern road that exactly follows the path of the Wade Road built in the eighteenth century to enable government troops to patrol the Highlands.

Newtonmore

The descent from Dalwhinnie through Glen Truim ends at Newtonmore, the start of a 15-mile stretch of more heavily populated terrain. As its name suggests, Newtonmore (meaning 'great new town') is relatively recent as a Highland town, first mentioned in government papers in 1823, but then boosted after 1862 by the railway to today's popula-tion of around 1,000. Those who alight from the train will find a main street with a range of stores serving both local residents and tourists; a 1929 town guide registered twenty businesses, includ-ing seven grocers, two butchers and seven apparel outlets.

Today, Newtonmore is known for its Highland Folk Museum, a reconstruction of an eighteenth-century township on a large plot just outside town. Various buildings – farm, shop, school – are spread out along a mile, including a station building called, fictionally, 'Aultlarie' after the local croft farm; it has been positioned next to a private crossing on the train line, which runs next to the museum.

WADE ROADS

In the wake of the Jacobite insurrections of 1715 and 1719, George I appointed George Wade (1673–1748) as Commander-in-Chief of North Britain with the remit to fortify the Highlands and suppress future rebellions. Wade's troops strengthened forts at Inverness, Fort William and Ruthven, but he became best known for his Romanesque long, straight, wide (16ft) roads through the mountains.

Between 1724 and 1734, Wade built four roads, of which the longest, at 99 miles, was from Dunkeld to Inverness, within a total of 300 miles. Ironically, stretches of Wade Roads would prove useful to the Jacobite rebels marching south under Bonnie Prince Charlie in 1745–46, so Wade retired rather ignominiously in 1747. Equally ironic was that his replacement as Commander-in-Chief was the Duke of Cumberland, who defeated the Bonnie Prince at Culloden in 1746.

Today, Wade Roads and those of his successor, Major William Caulfeild – who built another 800 miles of military road – are still in use either as metalled roads – as in Glen Truim – or as hiking or cycling trails. Meanwhile, Wade's name occurred in a little-sung verse of the British national anthem, God Save the King/Queen:

Lord, grant that Marshal Wade may, by Thy mighty aid, victory bring
May he sedition hush and, like a torrent, rush
Rebellious Scots to crush
God save the King

Southbound Highland Main Class 170 passing the Highland Folk Museum; note the museum's pet Shetland pony. In the background are the Cairngorm mountains.

'Aultlarie' station building next to the working level crossing at the Highland Folk Museum.

Newtonmore is also famous for the sport of shinty, or camanachd: this is a Highland team sport in which twelve players on either side use camans (similar to hockey sticks) to pass a small, hard ball, and score into goals at the end of an outdoor pitch. The ball can be played in the air, and rules for tackling and the use of the stick are looser than in field hockey, making for an exuberant game with a fair risk of injury!

The town's club has been a regular winner of the league and cup titles over the years (against arch-rival Kingussie, further up the Main Line). The Newtonmore club website gives detailed instructions for attending home matches by train. For the usual Saturday 'throw-up' at 14.30, travel details are as follows:

> …a southbound train stops in Newtonmore at 13.49 and the northbound at 13.09. …Walk up Station Road till the intersection with the B9150 (just over a quarter of a mile), then turn left and walk out of the village for 600 yards past Chef's Grill. The Eilan is on the right-hand side, and the walk will take you about 15 minutes.

Back at the station, Newtonmore's H-plan main building – similar to Pitlochry's – was converted and sold as a private house after Beeching rationalization in 1967: as Railscot contributor David Spaven put it: 'The station was de-staffed, the main building sold off, the platform shifted eastwards, the loop lifted and the signal box closed. Not much more to "rationalize" then!' Unusually, what Railscot calls an 'imitation signal box' was built near the line as a one-bedroomed holiday home.

Kingussie

Immediately after Newtonmore – passing the Highland Folk Museum – trains pull into Kingussie, which is slightly larger than its shinty rival (population 1,400) and served by trains in either direction much more frequently (including stops here by Caledonian Sleeper and LNER). An important demand for the service comes from Kingussie High School, adjacent to the station, whose buildings have been extended to accommodate a rising school roll (expected to reach 500 by 2020).

The station itself features, on the northbound side, a substantial canopied building from 1894, while the southbound platform has a shelter bearing a 'No Loitering' warning and an interesting piece of Highland railway history: the platform was raised to standard height in 2017, having previously been slightly lower to allow sheep or cattle to walk into their wagons. A portable step was kept on the platform for staff to help passengers aboard the southbound train.

A bird's-eye view of the area around Kingussie and Newtonmore shows that a major trunk road, the A86, forks off here from the A9 as the only such road leading west from the A9 between Pitlochry and Inverness. This shortage of east–west routes across the Highlands was not lost on early railway investors, who proposed a cross-country line from Newtonmore to join the West Highland Line – but this never materialized.

From Kingussie

Pulling out of Kingussie northbound, the train affords views to the spectacular ruins of Ruthven Barracks, perched on an earthwork rising high above the valley of the River Spey. The barracks were occupied in the eighteenth century by British government troops sent to suppress Jacobite rebellions.

The thirteen-minute run from Kingussie to Aviemore has a more populous, busier feel than earlier on the Main Line, as trains approach the 'playground of the Highlands', Aviemore. This stretch of the Spey valley offers tourist attractions such as 'working sheepdogs' at Leault Farm, several picnic and bird-watching spots (the Rothiemurchus Centre), and the Highland Wildlife Park. The line is now in the valley of the River Spey, with the Cairngorms towering up to the east and the Monadhliath mountains to the west. The population in the valley justifies three roads: the A9, the winding B970 Ruthven road, and the pretty B9152 through Kincraig, where there was a station until 1965 – the building is now a private house.

The ruins of Ruthven Barracks (Historic Environment Scotland) seen from rail and road (A9) near Kingussie. The early castles date from 1229 and 1451; they were rebuilt in the eighteenth century as barracks for government troops employed in suppressing the Jacobite rebellion.

Aviemore

Aviemore, the busiest resort town in the Highlands, has a population of 3,500 (up some 1,000 over twenty years). An inconspicuous village until the 1860s, its first railway station (built in 1863, on the Inverness & Perth Junction) put Aviemore on the map. Population growth accelerated in the 1890s when the Inverness & Aviemore Direct (by Highland Railway) opened, at which point Aviemore became a junction station with the Strathspey Railway, which headed north-east to Boat of Garten and Grantown-on-Spey (*see* previous chapter for coverage of the Strathspey line).

Tourism in Aviemore took off in the 1960s after a chairlift for skiers and walkers was added, and Aviemore became a destination for Scottish families on holiday, boosted by an indoor leisure centre added later in the decade.

Aviemore is a key destination for Highland Main users: 150,000 passengers pass through annually. It is a capacious station with a distinctive livery.

All Aboard! Aviemore Station

Situated at the southern entrance to the town's long commercial strip, Aviemore station is surrounded by hotels, restaurants, bars and shops focused mainly on outdoor gear or souvenirs. Originally built in 1863 for the line to Forres, it was extended for the arrival of the direct line to Inverness in 1892; both lines served Aviemore until closure of the Forres line under Beeching in 1965.

Rebuilding in 1998 made space for the heritage Strathspey Railway (*see* Lost Lines, later in this chapter) to use one of three platforms for its heritage steam trains. Buildings on the island platform were restored to offer Strathspey customers a waiting room, booking office, staff office, shop and toilets.

The main buildings fronting on Grampian Road contain facilities for ScotRail, a branch of WH Smith, the newsagent, also serving coffee, and a restaurant called The Highland Line.

From Aviemore

From Aviemore, the Main Line follows the path of the A9 northwards, while the A95 and B970 veer off eastwards – as does the restored part of the Strathspey line – for the 14 miles to Grantown-on-Spey. Tourist and outdoor activities are concentrated in this area, including Loch Morlich, Coylumbridge (large hotel and timeshare), the Rothiemurchus estate, and eventually the Cairngorm Mountain resort, one of five snow sports resorts in the Highlands. (A mile-long funicular railway at Cairngorm Mountain was closed indefinitely in 2019 due to structural problems.)

While leaving Aviemore by train to head north, the division of the line can still be seen within the town, the preserved line now tracked by the Speyside Way hiking route towards the north-east, while the Highland Main heads directly north for one more stop before Inverness at Carrbridge.

Carrbridge and Beyond

The village of Carrbridge, like Newtonmore, is only served a few times daily, although the Caledonian Sleeper (northbound) stops here. Carrbridge station (called Carr Bridge until 1983) is a half mile on foot from the centre of the village, which boasts what is claimed to be the oldest stone bridge in the Highlands (the Packhorse Bridge across River Dulnain, dated 1717); there is also the very popular modern family attraction, the Landmark Forest Adventure Park. Another Carrbridge claim to fame is the World Porridge-Making Championship, held in the village hall since 1994, the winner receiving a trophy in the shape of a spurtle (the traditional implement for stirring porridge).

After Carrbridge, there is another important climb on the Main Line, which, like the need to climb Drumochter, had inhibited early railway planning. (Apart from the engineering demands, there were few communities or industries to serve

An almost monochrome winter scene at Carrbridge station. SRPS

along this line.) At the hamlet of Slochd, a viaduct had to be built (over 100 feet high) just before the train reaches Slochd summit (1,315ft) – *see* photo earlier in this chapter.

The Findhorn Viaduct

Another viaduct was needed to cross the River Findhorn, which runs for 62 miles eastwards from the Monadhliath mountain range to reach the Moray Firth near Forres. (There is a separate railway viaduct over the river near Forres, also called Findhorn Viaduct.) The Findhorn Viaduct on the Main Line is a lattice steel bridge carried on eight stone piers, which taper upwards to a height of nearly 150ft above the river. (The viaduct makes for a magnificent sight from the A9, where travellers new to the area often mistake it for the famous Glenfinnan Viaduct of Harry Potter fame! – *see* Chapter 7.)

Tomatin and Beyond

Immediately after the Findhorn Viaduct, the line runs through the village of Tomatin and directly through the grounds of the distillery for which it is famous. (Tomatin means 'juniper hill': early illicit distilling was disguised by the burning of juniper bushes.) Until the closures of 1965, Tomatin had its own station and the distillery had its own spur and siding. Historically, the distillery opened in 1897,

coinciding with the railway era, although its raw materials and casks of whisky are now delivered by road. Owing to the distillery's isolation, thirty houses – visible from the train – were built for workers.

Moy

Leaving the distillery grounds, the railway line rejoins the path of the A9 to pass Loch Moy and the village of Moy, whose station was closed in 1965. Now a house, the station building included a private waiting room for the Mackintosh Clan Chief who lived in Moy Hall, on the shore of the nearby loch.

After Moy, the line diverts northwards from the A9 to Craggie, where there was a station until 1965 called Daviot, although it was nearly a mile from that village. From here, the line diverts even further from the A9 – which heads on a straight line northwestwards into Inverness – on a 10-mile eastward loop through the area known as Drummossie Muir (moor).

The Culloden Viaduct

The impressive Culloden railway viaduct stands on the eastern end of the loop through Drummossie; finished in 1898, it stretches for 600 yards on twenty-eight arches over the River Nairn, near to a site of ancient standing stones known as Clava Cairns. A

Culloden Viaduct passing through pasture. In the foreground, flowering thistles are beginning to fade in late summer.

BATTLE OF CULLODEN, DRUMMOSSIE MUIR, 17 APRIL 1746

The last battle on British soil took place on 17 April 1746 when British government troops, under the Duke of Cumberland, defeated the Jacobite rebels led by Bonnie Prince Charlie on a battlefield near the Highland village of Culloden, 6 miles from Inverness.

The pitched battle took place on a flat area of Drummossie Moor, which meant the Highland rebels were unable to use their usual battle tactics, such as the 'charge'. The heavy government artillery quickly killed up to 2,000 Jacobites, with only some fifty fatal casualties on the government side.

Visits to the National Trust for Scotland's battlefield centre have been boosted by the fictional *Outlander* series of books and television programmes, in which the heroic couple, Claire and Jamie, attempt to stop the 1745 rebellion and Culloden from happening.

BELOW: *Inverness station in summer 1906. Trains for Aberdeen are on the left, and for Wick on the right. Produced as a postcard for Highland Railway. SRPS*

station at the northern end of the viaduct, called Culloden Moor, was closed in 1965.

At the centre of the Drummossie loop, around which the viaduct curves, lies the Battlefield of Culloden visitor centre (National Trust for Scotland), an impressive post-modern structure that blends into the flat landscape.

Inverness

Passing through the village of Culloden itself, the line enters the suburbs of Inverness. At Milburn Junction, the Main Line crosses over the line from Aberdeen and then passes by Inverness TMD (traction maintenance depot), south of the station. A former shed here (in existence from 1855 to 1962, when it was demolished) was an impressive 'roundhouse', entered through a 'triumphal archway' (Railscot), capable of servicing up to a dozen steam locomotives. Maintenance is now carried out north of Inverness station at Lochgorm Works, which also date back to 1855; over forty locomotives were built at Lochgorm between 1869 and 1905 (Shed Bash UK).

Reception area at the Royal Highland Hotel, Inverness, showing the magnificent staircase that, by repute, was the inspiration for the grand staircase on RMS Titanic.

All Aboard! Inverness Station

As at Aberdeen, rail passengers arrive at a modernized station in Inverness, and can make their way out either straight into Eastgate, the city's modern shopping centre, or into the adjacent bus station. Although the 1968 remodelled frontage of Inverness station has few admirers, the station is, at least, right in the centre of the city – unlike those at many Highland towns.

As befits a hub station, there are seven long platforms at Inverness station, with trains arriving from Aberdeen, from Perth and the south and from Dingwall, a junction to the north of Inverness for trains from the Far North (Thurso and Wick) and the North West (the Kyle of Lochalsh line).

Emerging through the modern main entrance on to Academy Street, a busy thoroughfare, there are several visual reminders of Highland and railway history: the Royal Highland Hotel (1854), famous for its magnificent staircase, abuts the station building; on the opposite side of Station Square, the entrance to Highland Rail House, now containing serviced offices to let, was originally railway property; and the forecourt boasts a statue to the 79th Queen's Own Cameron Highlanders regiment, added in 1893.

Inverness station is due to undergo another overhaul (worth £6m, expected to start in 2020), having been extended and remodelled several times in its history; the station was originally built (in 1855) for the Inverness & Nairn company, long before there was a line to the south.

Modern Inverness

For many tourists, Inverness acts as a short stop-over en route to visiting the area's two most popular attractions: the Battlefield of Culloden and, of course, the hunt for the legendary Loch Ness monster, 'Nessie'!

Modern Inverness has been expanding steadily. When the first railways were built, the town had a population of under 20,000, a figure that had doubled by the year 2000, when city status was granted; it is now approaching 70,000. The opening of a University of the Highlands & Islands has given the city a more vibrant, youthful air than it once had, coupled with European Union development finance and a thriving tourism market.

Lost Lines: To Grantown-on-Spey and Forres

As introduced in the previous chapter covering developments in the Grampians, two early lines reached the vicinity of today's Main Line, both emanating from Grantown-on-Spey, 14 miles to the east of Aviemore.

Inverness & Perth Junction

Inverness & Perth Junction was the 'long way round' to reach the south from Inverness until the technology and finance were in place to build across Drumochter and Slochd. Building a line south of Forres in 1863 was seen as a convenience for reaching the south, since it passed through 15 miles of thinly populated rural territory before reaching Grantown-on-Spey. However, the line was certainly useful for transporting farm produce and fish from the Moray coast.

From Forres, the line heading south served the Dallas Dhu distillery – which ceased production in 1983 but remains open as a whisky museum – and then stopped at hamlets or halts such as Rafford, Dunphail and Dava. At Dunphail, cattle were gathered and loaded for the south at a long platform; near here, an impressive viaduct (still standing) had to be built to cross the River Divie, with a total length of nearly 500 feet over seven arches. Another challenge was the climb to Dava Summit (1,050ft), although the gradients were not severe.

Today, the line is largely preserved as the 24-mile Dava Way, a trail promoted by the Dava Way Association (founded in 1997, the way opened in 2005) for walkers and cyclists.

The Strathspey Railway

Also in 1863, the Strathspey Railway reached Grantown-on-Spey, from where both lines headed off on separate lines in a south-westerly direction with the aim of connecting to southbound lines, through Broomhill and then diverging at Boat of Garten (nowadays a station on the preserved Strathspey Railway). Although these early railways through Grampian were significant in their era, they closed in 1965, leaving only two routes to Inverness: from Aberdeen passing through Forres and up the 'backbone' line from Perth over the Drumochter Pass (Inverness & Aviemore Direct, built in the 1890s).

The Strathspey Railway Association celebrated 'forty years of Highland steam' in 2018, a period in which it has acquired or leased six steam engines. Strathspey's Standard Service runs three times daily in summer from Aviemore to Boat of Garten and a halt (and reconstructed station) at Broomhill. There are Specials throughout the year including Dining on Board, Whisky Tasting and Santa Express.

The majority of Strathspey services are hauled by LMS 2-6-0 no. 46512 (built in 1952, and resumed service in 2011). The Association effectively has its own station, shared with the modern station at Aviemore (profiled earlier in this chapter). There are ambitions to reconnect the line with Grantown – the 'Rails to Grantown' project – and volunteers have begun preparatory work.

Services on the Highland Main Line

In 2019, ScotRail referred to the Highland Main Line but its relevant timetable was published as 'Edinburgh & Glasgow–Inverness', with the following services running between 20 May and 8 December:

- Glasgow to Inverness. Mon.–Sat.: Five daily, stopping at nearly all the stations described above. Sun.: Three services. Other services requiring changes at Perth

The Santa Express, the annual special on Strathspey hauled by LMS 2-6-0 no. 46512. Note the uniformed guards and the elfish 'helper'!

- Edinburgh to Inverness. Mon.–Sat.: Five daily via Fife stations to Perth. Sun.: Three services. Other services requiring changes at Perth

A daily LNER service from London stopped at Edinburgh (16.34), Stirling, Gleneagles, Perth (17.58), Pitlochry, Kingussie and Aviemore arr. Inverness 20.04

During 2019, high-speed trains were introduced and frequency increased on the line; some journeys from the Central Belt to Inverness had their times reduced to three hours and two minutes, a gain of about fifteen minutes on previous best times.

Sources for the Highland Main Line

(*See also* Sources chapter for general sources.)

The History of the Railways of the Scottish Highlands (series 1977–1990):
> Originally published by David & Charles, now from House of Lochar, Isle of Colonsay
> Chapter 2, Vallance, H.A., *The Highland Railway*

Christopher, J. and McCutcheon, C., *Locomotives of the Highland Railway* (Amberley 2014)

Fenwick, K., *The Highland Railway (Britain in Old Photographs)* (The History Press 2009)

Hogg, C. and Patrick, L., *Scottish Railway Icons: The Highlands* (Amberley 2019)

Ross, D., *The Highland Railway* (Stenlake 2005)

Sinclair, N., *The Highland Main Line* (Atlantic Transport 1998)

Sinclair, N., *Highland Railway: People and Places* (Breedon Books 2005)

Thomas, J. and Turnock, D., *A Regional History of the Railways of Great Britain Vol 15: The North of Scotland* (David & Charles 1989)

Internet (www.)

Highland Main Line Community Rail Partnership (highlandmainlinecrp.co.uk)

Highland Railway Society (hrsoc.org.uk)

Network Rail (networkrail.co.uk) – page about 'Highland Main Line'

Railscot.co.uk – primary resource for Scottish railway information

ScotRail (ScotRail.co.uk) – official website of Abellio franchise

scot-rail (scot-rail.co.uk) – 'Scotland's online rail enthusiast community'

Strathspey Railway (strathspeyrailway.co.uk) – Strathspey Railway Association

CHAPTER 5

A Duke's Legacy: the Far North Line

Strange as it may seem today, it was a duke and a landowner who inspired the creation of a railway running through miles of largely deserted landscape that still exists today as the Far North Line (though where exactly 'north' starts in Scotland is often a matter of conjecture). The line runs from Dingwall (after leaving the railway hub at Inverness) to both Thurso and Wick on the far north-east coast of the Scottish mainland.

As a nineteenth-century dukedom, Sutherland stretched from Dornoch up the eastern coast to Helmsdale, and across an enormous area in the far north-west of the Scottish mainland, much of it under the control of the dukedom. In 1800, the land in question was an estate stretching for 1.5 million acres, one of the largest private

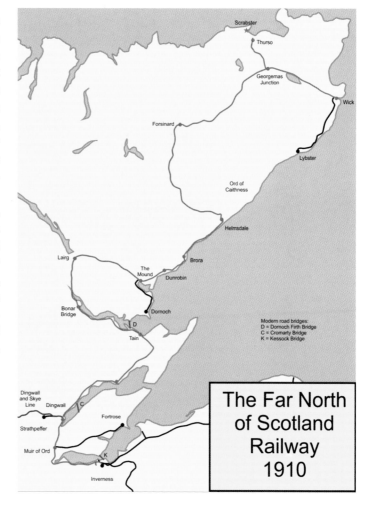

A 1910 map of the Far North Line from Inverness to Thurso and Wick, including inland 'loops' to Lairg and Forsinard. Muir of Ord to Fortrose and Dornoch and Lybster branches no longer exist. WIKIMEDIA COMMONS

estates in Europe. The 1st Duke, George Granville Leveson-Gower, was elevated to that title by King William IV in 1833; considered one of the wealthiest men in Britain, the Duke was implicated in the worst of the 'clearances' of peasants from their lands in the early part of the century (*see* section 'The Clearances', below).

The 2nd Duke (1786–1861) developed the family seat in Scotland, Dunrobin Castle, into the fairytale castle, which, when opened to the public, would become a magnetic attraction for tourists travelling through this part of Scotland. His son, the 3rd Duke (George Sutherland Leveson-Gower, 1828 to 1892) was a rail enthusiast who sponsored both the public Sutherland Railway and his own private railway (the Duke of Sutherland's), later helping to found the Highland Railway (which worked the Sutherland railways).

Earlier family members had invested in Liverpool & Manchester, and the 3rd Duke was already a director of London & North West – and a railway engineering enthusiast – long before the chance to build in Sutherland came up. He also became a director of Highland Railway.

The Clearances

The clearance of peasants from the land would obviously have some impact on land management by the great landowners, including decisions on road and rail development through the estates. In the early decades of the nineteenth century, great Scottish (and sometimes English) landowners were associated with this phase of economic history, when tenant families were often brutally removed, or 'cleared' from agricultural land, primarily to make way for sheep farming. Renting to 'cottars' or crofters had become less profitable than raising sheep. Some 15,000 people were cleared from the land, with such brutality that the name of the factor employed by the Sutherlands, Patrick Sellar, later became synonymous with those brutal evictions, which peaked around 1820.

Later in the nineteenth century, landlords also cleared their estates to repopulate them with game (deer or grouse), in order to entertain their wealthy friends on hunting and shooting holidays. Famine during the potato blight also contributed to migration from the Highlands, and there could even be positive reasons for families to leave behind their ancestral lands: the chance to join the industrial revolution in southern Scotland, or to migrate overseas for opportunities in the expanding British Empire.

The landlords were not universally evil: some rehoused their tenants in purpose-built rural villages, or even by the sea, in the vain hope that the peasant farmers would train themselves to become sea fishermen! So-called assisted passages were also provided, the financial assistance coming in the form of a one-way ticket out of the Highlands.

The Duke's Railway

Although it was the brainchild of the 3rd Duke of Sutherland to have his own railway, some background from further south is needed in order to understand how the Far North Line eventually evolved and survived.

The 1850s had seen Inverness connected to Aberdeen, and a flurry of privately owned railways opening up in the Central Highlands and Grampian. The northward push started in 1862 with the Inverness & Ross-shire line (from Inverness to Dingwall), but that would be absorbed in quick succession by the Inverness & Aberdeen Junction, and then subsumed under Highland Railway in 1865. By then, Dingwall had been connected to the port of Invergordon (in 1863).

Five years later, in 1868, Sutherland Railway opened between Bonar Bridge and Golspie, with the 3rd Duke as a major shareholder. To extend the line north to Helmsdale, an Act for the distinctively titled 'Duke of Sutherland's Railway' was passed; by the time that line was up and running across the Duke's estate, he had invested in Caithness Railway and then Caithness & Sutherland (along with investment from Highland Railway, which would take over the whole Far North eventually, in 1884).

Fairy-tale turrets on Dunrobin Castle overlooking the North Sea – the region's number one tourist destination. ISTOCK.COM/JULE BERLIN

Ultimate Destinations on the Far North

The Far North connects mostly small towns and villages, with three notable exceptions: Invergordon, an industrial port; Dunrobin Castle, the seat of the Duke of Sutherland; and Dornoch, a popular and salubrious coastal resort and golfing destination (although, ironically, the direct rail loop to Dornoch was closed in 1966).

The most important destinations on the line are therefore its termini at Thurso and Wick. And many Far North passengers enjoying the views across inland Sutherland and Caithness – sometimes of a bleak, empty landscape – are ultimately bound for destinations beyond Thurso and Wick. Thurso is the gateway for ferries to the Orkney Islands, and in recent years, a calling point on the rapidly developed touring route known as the 'North Coast 500'. Wick is primarily a working town rather than a tourist destination, but arrivals at its station may be heading (by bus) for John O'Groats, the most northern village in Britain.

The Far North: Station by Station

A Historic Journey from Inverness to Thurso and Wick

> Venture north from Inverness, tracing the North Sea coast past distilleries, salmon rivers and golf courses to Thurso and the once-mighty fishing port of Wick.
> ScotRail website promoting the Far North Line

Far North trains start in the former counties of Inverness-shire and Ross-shire (which gave their name to pioneering railway companies), and then into what were once the large, semi-independent regions known as Sutherland and Caithness. The name 'Caithness' probably derives from the 'cat people' of Pictish tribal origin; it was an earldom from the fourteenth century, and the current duke – the 20th – is a hereditary peer in the House of Lords, and chief of Clan Sinclair. Sutherland was the 'south land' of Norse rulership from the eighth

to the fifteenth centuries; the dukedom was created for a noble of English origin, so unusually, this dukedom in the peerage of the United Kingdom has no historic clan chieftainship or peerage within Scotland.

The distance covered by the Far North Line is impressive enough in a Scottish (or even British) context. The journey totals three hours fifteen minutes from Inverness to Wick. For example, to reach Wick by mid-afternoon (according to the timetable at the time of writing, at 14.56h), passengers from Glasgow would have to make an early start (7.07h). The train would allow a twelve-minute stop at Inverness before boarding the Far North Line, making for a total journey time of just under seven hours from Glasgow to Wick, with calls at up to thirty-three stations (including request stops on the Far North).

Two termini are given in the timetable: Thurso and Wick. At Georgemas Junction, the train pauses before reversing to reach Thurso on the north coast, and then comes back through Georgemas to reach Wick, on the east coast.

Inverness to Dingwall

The Highland capital, Inverness, sits at the mouth of the River Ness, which is a run-off from Loch Ness; the Caledonian Canal also reaches the sea at Inverness. Both river and canal empty into the estuary known as the Beauly Firth, whose waters in turn flow eastwards into the larger Moray Firth, eventually spilling out into the North Sea. These estuaries were barriers to travel by road until the building of the Kessock Bridge (opened in 1982), which crosses where the two firths meet.

When the Kessock Bridge was planned, building a dual road and rail bridge was soon discounted for two reasons: the physical logistics, with high winds a constant danger, and the economic era in which it was proposed – the 1970s, when 'the car was king', and Beeching rationalizations were beginning to bite. In retrospect, retaining the 'loop' along the Beauly Firth to Dingwall has proved worthwhile, this line connecting Inverness with popular towns for both commuters and tourists (Beauly, Muir of Ord, Conon Bridge, Maryburgh and Dingwall, the latter also the junction for the Kyle Line to the west).

Leaving Inverness station, the Far North passes through industrial estates, and crosses the River Ness on a simple, low viaduct built to replace the 1862 viaduct, which had collapsed in the great flood of 1989. Railscot describes the new viaduct as 'elegant, simple and unremarkable'. Then the train crosses the Caledonian Canal – just before the canal empties into the Beauly Firth – and runs along the south bank of the firth, parallel to the A862.

Beauly, and Beyond

A small viaduct over the narrows of the River Beauly takes the train into the town of Beauly itself, fifteen minutes out of Inverness. A pretty and prosperous town, surrounded by good farmland, Beauly (with a population of 1,164) is best known for its ruined priory, built for Valliscaulian monks in the thirteenth century. The original station closed in 1960, almost exactly a century after the first one opened, but local campaigning helped to reopen it in 2002. Campaigners claim that 75 per cent of Beauly commuters switched from road to rail as a result of their efforts, despite some difficulty in boarding the trains: Beauly has officially the shortest platform in Britain, just 49.4ft in length, so passengers board and alight through the one central door. (The platform at Conon Bridge, two stops north on the Far North Line, is marginally longer at 49.5ft, while Dilton Marsh, in Wiltshire, is a close rival.)

Conon Bridge

As part of reviving this railway line, a similarly modest reopening of a station took place further north at Conon Bridge (population 2,000), where the line skirts around Loch Conon to avoid the need for a bridge.

The revived station (from 1860 originally) opened in 2013 with a single platform marginally longer than Beauly's, and a helpful sign advising passengers not to alight into the bushes on the offside of the train!

Muir of Ord

Before reaching Conon Bridge, the northbound trains from Inverness call at Muir of Ord (population 3,000), known for its Diageo-owned whisky distillery: its public tours benefit from the fact that Muir of Ord has the only distillery for many miles around. The station was closed in 1960, but was reinstated in 1976.

Locals consider Muir of Ord to be part of the mysteriously named Black Isle – a peninsula that is neither black nor an island – which stretches 25 miles eastwards from here towards the North Sea, flanked by the firths of Cromarty and Moray. The predominantly rural Black Isle was once served by a branch line running from Muir of Ord to Fortrose (*see* the section 'Lost Lines in the North of Scotland', below in this chapter).

Dingwall, and Beyond

Just over half an hour from Inverness, the Far North pulls into Dingwall, which also serves the Kyle Line,

DMU 158708 due to depart Dingwall, the junction for the Kyle and Far North lines. Behind the glazed canopy are the ticket office and Tina's Tearoom.

making it one of the few junction stations in the Highlands. Formerly the county town of Ross-shire, Dingwall's resident population (5,500) is swelled temporarily when its football club, Ross County, is playing at home: Victoria Park stadium is a four-minute walk from the railway station. 'The Staggies' maintain an intense rivalry with Inverness Caledonian Thistle FC, the only other Highland club to have played in the top tier of Scottish football.

All Aboard! Dingwall Station

The station at Dingwall is the interchange for westbound and northern routes from Inverness. The main station is a handsome, late Victorian building in red sandstone – 'HR 1886' is inscribed in stone above one window – with a pitched slate roof, crow-step gabling and several chimneys, a reminder that the waiting room would have offered a warming coal fire.

Today, the station building houses the equally welcoming Tina's Tearoom, serving down-to-earth fare such as bacon rolls, beans on toast or coronation chicken salad.

Also at the station is a popular pub for locals with a steam theme (the Mallard Bar), and there is also a Christian bookshop. An adjacent private dwelling still bears the name 'Station House'.

Alness

Leaving behind Dingwall station and its cosy tearoom, the Far North journey is immediately rewarding, the train running close by the Cromarty Firth – with the chance of spotting seabirds or

Murals at Invergordon station – 'The Long Goodbye', by Tracey Shough – commemorating the Seaforth Highlanders' use of the station in World War II.

perhaps seals – before pulling into quiet Alness station (closed 1960, re-opened 1973).

Invergordon

Six minutes later, the train pulls through very different scenery into Invergordon: industrial buildings and associated branch lines for freight, whisky warehouses (Whyte & Mackay), a housing estate, and other visible evidence of Invergordon's heritage as a working town and port. Oil rigs and wind turbines have been made or repaired here, and Invergordon was once a Royal Navy base – infamous for a rare strike by sailors, the Invergordon Mutiny, in 1931 – but in modern times the warships have been replaced by cruise ships, disembarking tourists for coach tours of the Highlands. The station itself has murals commemorating the soldiers based here.

Fearn

Back in open countryside, the line soon moves inland from the coast of the firth to pause at Fearn, a curious survivor of cutbacks given its rural location and distance (over a mile) from the nearest villages.

To the south of the station, however, a B road leads to the Nigg Ferry, which connects this area to the town of Cromarty at the tip of the Black Isle; a summer service run by Highland Council, the ferry itself carries twelve passengers and just two vehicles.

Tain

Tain, the next stop, is a more substantial one, serving a population of 3,590. The main employer is the Glenmorangie distillery, producing a globally recognized single malt brand, which is also the top single malt in the Scottish market. The station once boasted an engine shed, turntable and water tower.

Up to this point, the railway has followed fairly closely the line of the northbound trunk road, the A9, but the routes diverge at the next geographical barrier to ground transport, the Dornoch Firth (the fourth firth seen on this journey from Inverness). To cross the firth, an impressive road bridge was completed in 1991 (nine years after the Kessock Bridge at Inverness) to carry the A9, but the railway line turns inland, avoiding the firth. The proposal to

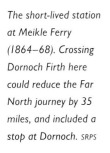

The short-lived station at Meikle Ferry (1864–68). Crossing Dornoch Firth here could reduce the Far North journey by 35 miles, and included a stop at Dornoch. SRPS

make the bridge dual use (rail and road) was turned down on economic grounds, although it would have cut forty-five minutes from the Far North journey time. Historically, a busy ferry had operated across the Dornoch Firth, although it made tragic news in 1809 when 99 of its 111 passengers drowned as the crowded ferry overturned. Formerly a station called Meikle Ferry served the ferry, but only from 1864 to 1868.

Ardgay, and Beyond

So instead of crossing the firth, the Far North continues its journey on a long loop through thinly populated areas of Sutherland, rather than heading into Dornoch, the former county town (*see* section 'Lost Lines in the North of Scotland', below). The line hugs the south side of the firth all the way to its next stop at Ardgay, which, until 1977, was named Bonar Bridge. This change finally corrected an historical anomaly: although 'Inverness to Bonar Bridge' was proclaimed proudly in 1864 as the original exten-sion of the line from Invergordon, the station was in Ardgay, a mile away from Bonar Bridge. (The optimistic naming of stations, relative to their actual locations, was not uncommon on early Highland lines, a practice sometimes echoed in the European airport locations of modern 'budget' airlines!)

From Ardgay, the train crosses a small viaduct into Bonar Bridge itself, lying at the top of the Dornoch Firth, into which flow four rivers. The line travels close to the historic border between the old counties of Sutherland and Ross & Cromarty (now part of Highland Council area).

Culrain

Only four minutes beyond Ardgay is a request stop at sleepy Culrain village, adjacent to which is the site of the Battle of Carbisdale in 1650, with Carbisdale Castle half a mile to the north (*see* panel).

Culrain was a stop for backpackers and youth groups using Carbisdale Castle when it was a hostel, from 1945 to 2014; then it was bought privately for commercial redevelopment.

Invershin

Carbisdale could also be accessed from Invershin, the next station, which is just half a mile away across the Kyle of Sutherland, making it one of the shortest journeys between stations on the UK network. Assuming the train stops at both stations, which are 'request' stops, the journey lasts less than two minutes. In fact Culrain to Invershin is not the only short journey on this line: this is a notable feature of the Far North, compared to long distances between stations on other Highland lines. Further north, Golspie to Dunrobin takes just two minutes.

The short transit to Invershin is occupied by crossing the handsome Oykel (or Shin) Viaduct across the Kyle. Opened in 1868, the unusual 230ft long viaduct uses masonry arches on the river banks, across which a lattice girder carries the railway track; since the track runs on top of the girder structure rather than within it, clear views of the river and Carbisdale Castle are afforded for passengers. For walkers and cyclists, a footbridge was built on the side of the viaduct in 2000.

CARBISDALE: THE SITE OF TWO BATTLES

In 1650 at Carbisdale, a Royalist force under James Graham, 1st Marquis of Montrose, was defeated by rebellious supporters of the National Covenant, signed by Scottish Presbyterians in opposition to the Crown's imposition of a new church liturgy and prayer book. Hundreds of soldiers may have died attempting to swim across the waterway known as the Kyle of Sutherland.

Lands including the battlefield (53 acres in total) were offered for sale in 2019, comprising heather moor, pine woodland and open burns.

Carbisdale Castle was the site of a different type of battle. The forty-room castle was completed in 1917 for Mary Blair, the second wife of the 3rd Duke of Sutherland, the original creator of the Far North Line (see The Duke's Railway, section above). Following the Duke's death in 1892 and a dispute over his will, 'Duchess Blair' was allowed to build her own home on the Sutherland estate, but well away from the family seat at Dunrobin Castle.

The so-called 'Castle of Spite' naturally contains ghosts – a 'lady in white' and a 'hooded gardener'. Notably it also has external clocks on only three faces of its tower, and not on the one facing Dunrobin, reputedly because Duchess Blair refused to 'give the time of day' to her enemies at Dunrobin.

Invershin station buildings in a ruinous state in 2019. Note the old waiting hut, but the brand new LED customer information screen.

Reaching the north side of the Kyle, a steep path leads to the back entrance of Invershin station, where the main building is now a ruin. Part of the platform was, equally rarely, made of timber boards rather than stone or concrete.

After Invershin, the line runs directly north on the bank above the River Shin, with a glimpse of the Falls of Shin outdoor attraction within Shin Forest. The original visitor centre burned down in 2013, but ownership passed to a local trust, which raised £1.4m for a rebuilt centre, opened in 2017.

Lairg

The next stop is at Lairg (with 900 residents), a compulsory stop although situated 2 miles south of the town centre. The self-proclaimed Crossroads of the North, the town sits at the southern end of Loch Shin with roads radiating outwards to the north coast (the A836 to Tongue, and the A838 to Durness), the west (the A839/837 to Assynt) as well

as south, with the railway, back to Inverness. Also an important market town, Lairg hosts Europe's largest annual sheep auction, and every August, the century-old Crofters' Show, when farming families compete in Highland activities such as throwing the wellie (or the haggis), cow judging and even sheep racing!

From Lairg, the line loops back south-eastwards to regain the coast. If no stop is requested at Rogart, the twenty-five-minute run from Lairg to Golspie through Strath Fleet is uneventful if scenic, bypassing several small villages.

Rogart

At Rogart, a railway enthusiast family operates an unusual eighteen-bed hostel called Sleeperzzz, using converted railway carriages right next to the station itself. Available from March to October, the accommodation is promoted as being ideal for 'folk looking to escape for some peace and tran-

Rogart station: holiday lets in coaches, and a collection of railway memorabilia in landscaped grounds ('Sleeperzzz', run by Kate and Frank Roach).

quillity'. The accommodation and the station itself are surrounded by a collection of Highland railway memorabilia.

After Rogart, the line follows the River Fleet, which runs into Loch Fleet, a compact, tidal basin (and a seawater loch) preserved as a nature reserve by the Scottish Wildlife Trust for birds, pine martens and 'rare woodland plants such as one-flowered wintergreens'. Alongside the loch, the line then starts to curve northwards, passing Mound Rock, a prominent cliff. (A former station near here, The Mound, was a junction for the Dornoch Light Railway: *see* section 'Lost Lines in the North of Scotland', below.)

Golspie, and Beyond

A straighter run after Mound Rock enables engines to reach maximum line speed on the 3-mile run towards Golspie (population 1,560), a 'planned' village of the early nineteenth century (*see* panel). Fronting on to the platform at Golspie is Station House, a four-bedroom conversion of the 1868 building, available to let as holiday accommodation.

The conversion uses the former ticket office as its sitting room and dining area, and retains the open fire.

GOLSPIE: A PLANNED VILLAGE

The planned villages created in the late eighteenth and early nineteenth centuries mainly housed crofters who were being 'cleared' from the land – in Golspie's case from the estate of the 1st Duke of Sutherland. At Golspie, families were given land to build their own houses (each restricted to 50 by 20 feet), together with a plot of farmland and use of the common cow pasture. A jetty was built for mooring fishing boats, since the purpose of the village was to encourage fishing for herring.

The Golspie project was overseen by Elizabeth, Duchess of Sutherland, who, for complex inheritance reasons, was also 19th Countess of Sutherland in her own right (*suo jure*). In 2019, the 24th Countess (also Elizabeth, born in 1921) owns the Sutherland estates, including Dunrobin Castle, separately from the continuing Dukedom of Sutherland. (Francis Egerton, born 1940, is the 7th Duke.)

Golspie has a controversial reminder of the Clearances: the town is overlooked by a 100-foot statue of the 1st Duke of Sutherland, although its inscription proclaims that it was erected out of gratitude by a 'mourning tenantry' for a 'kind and liberal landlord'.

Dunrobin Castle

After Golspie, the train will travel for less than two minutes before slowing to stop at the seasonal request stop for Dunrobin Castle. The private station serving Dunrobin was built in 1870, and later (1902) improved with the addition of a Swiss chalet-styled waiting room and a long platform for the many guests arriving by train to visit the duke. Inside, local and railway memorabilia are displayed (for group visits).

Like many Scottish castles, Dunrobin had several phases of expansion, evolving from a fortress into a symbol of wealth with major modifications for the 2nd Duke by Sir Charles Barry – architect for the Palace of Westminster – and by Sir Robert Lorimer after World War I. The spectacular castle is the most popular tourist attraction by far in this region of Scotland. In 2018, over 112,000 visited the castle, a number that has risen by two-thirds over five years; but only around one thousand rail passengers use Dunrobin station annually.

Brora

Brora is another unassuming town on this coast, but one with an unusual industrial heritage. Coal mining, rare in the Highlands, dated back to the sixteenth century and was used in salt panning for preserving fish during the decades of boom in herring fishing. (One of Scotland's primitive rail

Unique half-timbered private waiting room at Dunrobin Castle station.

tracks was built here, connecting the coal mine and the harbour with a horse-drawn cart and wooden rail track.) Woollen textile production was once important – Hunter's of Brora survives as a brand – and whisky distilling was initiated in 1819 by the 1st Duke. The two distilleries (Brora and Clynelish) have been revived by their owner, Diageo, which is also creating a modern visitor centre at Clynelish.

Beyond Brora

The 10-mile run to Helmsdale runs very close to the North Sea coast – at times, a few yards from the beach – alongside the A9 trunk road. Oil rigs and tankers may be spotted out at sea, while inland there are glimpses of ruined stone buildings, some of which have simply fallen out of use, while others are grim reminders of where pre-Clearance families might have eked out a living. (Still others

were built to house navvies building the railway and its stations, or for maintenance workers once the line was complete.) With so few settlements of any size in this region, it becomes clear on this run that financing a railway here was partly a charitable venture by the 3rd Duke.

Helmsdale

Rail passengers passing through, or alighting at the next station, Helmsdale, will immediately notice that the main building fronting on to the platform is now a holiday let. The station is on the other side of the River Helmsdale from the town centre, so passengers stopping here take a four-minute walk across Thomas Telford's pretty masonry bridge (1809).

Helmsdale's population is usually 700, but doubles during its Highland Games in August. The Time-

Helmsdale on the Far North Line. The station is on the left (south) side of Telford road bridge to the town centre; note the clock tower on the war memorial, and the gorse and broom in flower in June. ISTOCK.COM/CLAUDINE VM

Span cultural centre offers an insight into the area's history (the Clearances, fishing, a gold rush, and the extermination of the wolf!) and includes a reconstructed nineteenth-century street.

Beyond Helmsdale

Instead of continuing to Wick with the A9, the railway turns inland at Helmsdale to climb gently up Strath Kildonan (or Strath Ullie) – once a gold-panning valley – rather than negotiate the switchbacks built for the A9 up the jagged coastal route.

If no requests are made to stop at Kildonan or Kinbrace, it will be an uninterrupted, thirty-four-minute journey to Forsinard, all the while running parallel to the A897, a lonely A road through this remote region. Kildonan was incorporated into the line only to serve a nearby shooting lodge, while at Kinbrace, the narrow B871 forks off westward as the only side road off the A897, eventually reaching the north coast at Bettyhill.

Forsinard, and Beyond

Seven miles north of Kinbrace, Forsinard village is known for its Forsinard Flows bird reserve (managed by the Royal Society for the Protection of Birds). 'Flows' refers to a 50,000 area of blanket bog, across which fly golden plover, dunlin, greenshanks, skylarks, meadow pipits and hen harriers. The RSPB uses Forsinard station building as its HQ for the Flows, while nearby there is also an impressive, modern viewing tower to visit.

From Forsinard, a nineteenth-century proposal to continue the Far North through Strath Halladale to reach the north coast, 15 miles away, never materialized. Instead, while the A897 does continue northwards, the railway diverts 90 degrees to the east and the train will travel steadily uphill for twenty-four minutes (if no requests to stop are made at Altnabreac or Scotscalder) towards Georgemas Junction.

Stretches of this line are through pure wilderness, with no roads or evidence of inhabitation to be seen. The line crosses the historic county (or shire) boundary from Sutherland into Caithness; both names were incorporated into the original stretches of railway that came to make up the Far North Line. Local government reorganization relegated these county names under the Highland Council area, now managed from Inverness as the Council Area of Caithness, Sutherland and Easter Ross.

Close to the request stop of Altnabreac is the highest point on the Far North Line, 708 feet above sea level, 130 miles out of Inverness. The bleak outlook on a winter journey recalls the incident of January 1978 when a train was stranded for twenty hours during a blizzard that derailed four of the five coaches. Next day, the seventy passengers were airlifted by helicopter from Altnabreac to Wick.

After passing through Altnabreac, requests to stop at Scotscalder are equally rare, and trains no longer stop at the village of Halkirk (the station closed in 1960) so they usually stop next at Georgemas Junction. Railscot notes the 'curious' case of the

RAILWAY STATION CONVERSION

The station at Helmsdale features an unusual accommodation opportunity on a Scottish railway line, this time a conversion of the building – fronting on to the southbound platform – that used to hold offices, waiting rooms and the stationmaster's home. In 2013, after twenty-five years of dereliction, it opened as a self-catering cottage, with the difference that the rebuilding was funded by a community project involving rail enthusiasts. All proceeds go towards 'station improvements and promoting the Far North Line', and generally promoting tourism in East Sutherland.

The cottage at Helmsdale has four bedrooms and offers discounts to those arriving by public transport (or on foot or bicycle), the argument being that 'such groups are more likely to support local shops and amenities'. Uniquely, an additional discount is offered to cottage users who volunteer a half-day of their stay helping to maintain the station grounds.

The Helmsdale cottage is listed on RailwayStationCottages.co.uk, a 'hub for railway enthusiasts to find the perfect holidays'. In 2019, the site listed over forty UK properties, of which eight were in Scotland, seven of them in the Highlands: at Helmsdale, Golspie, Pitlochry ('Lineside'), Bridge of Orchy ('Taransay'), Duirinish ('Station Cottage') and Plockton ('Off The Rails').

TRAIN...SPOTTING? WILDLIFE AND LIVESTOCK SEEN IN THE HIGHLANDS

What wildlife can passengers hope to spot through the windows of Highland railway carriages? There is never a guarantee of spotting large wildlife other than birds in a landscape, which, despite its apparent wildness, has been tamed by man over many centuries. But the most likely candidates – among larger mammals – are the following:

- deer, both red and roe
- squirrels (grey, or occasionally red), rabbits and (more rarely) hares
- badgers, pine martens, voles and evidence of moles
- otter
- the Scottish wildcat
- feral goats

Bird watching is more rewarding, the Highland landscape being suited to raptors such as buzzards, kestrels, eagles, ospreys, harriers and other birds of prey. Along some rural lines, hedgerow and field birds are common, together with pheasants and grouse that have survived the shooting season.

Along coasts and lochs, water birds are too numerous to list, while seals, dolphins, whales and even some sharks come close to Scottish shores.

Livestock are dominated by sheep (over ten million of them), principally Cheviot and Scottish Blackface breeds, with cattle common on lower grazing. Pictures of Highland cows are sought after by visitors – and a postcard theme. Llamas from Peru are seen more often now: they deter foxes from attacking sheep.

Horses were once seen everywhere until their 'working' role was subverted by motor vehicles, but they are used for pony trekking in the Highlands. Scotland was the origin of some famous horse breeds: the Shetland and Highland pony, and the Clydesdale.

Forsinard station: the building is used by the RSPB. Note the disused signal box beyond the small, modern shelter and information boards.
WIKIMEDIA COMMONS

Bleak scene at lonely Altnabreac, looking south. Note the handcart and phone box. SRPS

station at Halkirk, which, although its population of 950 was substantial for this region, was closed while a station survived at Scotscalder that was the least used on the Far North Line.

Georgemas

Just under three hours, thirty minutes since leaving Inverness, Far North trains pause for four minutes at Georgemas and then reverse to head north on the branch line for Thurso. The same train, having reached Thurso after a ten-minute ride, pauses there for three minutes to let passengers disembark, and then returns (forwards, heading south-east) to Georgemas Junction. After another pause at the Junction, the service has a final seventeen-minute run before ending at Wick.

As a technical note on this anomalous 'return' journey involving Georgemas Junction, passengers for Wick can only stay on the train from Georgemas to Thurso and back thanks to an 'easement' of regulations in the National Routeing Guide (produced by the Rail Delivery Group). Officially, point-to-point passengers are going 'off route' by staying on the train as it moves backwards. Positive Easement

no. 81 states: 'Journeys to Wick may double back between Thurso and Georgemas Junction. This easement applies in both directions.'

Thurso

The train ride to the terminus at Thurso is through pleasant countryside, much of the way close to the gentle River Thurso.

With a population of 8,000 – only 3,000 when the railway first arrived – Thurso is an important regional centre for Caithness. An unusual local employer over the last sixty years has been the Dounreay nuclear plant, although it has been going through decommissioning since 2005. (Near Wick, a new study centre called Nucleus: the Nuclear and Caithness Archive, offers an unusual combination of local county history with the records of the Nuclear Decommissioning Authority.)

Passengers arriving in Thurso by rail may stay in one of the town's traditionally styled hotels (The Station Hotel itself, or The Pentland or The Royal), and can visit Caithness Horizons, an excellent modern museum and art gallery. But visitors are more likely to use Thurso as a base for travelling

Georgemas Junction from the east in 1967: the station building survives, but the island platform (and the flower beds) has long gone.
JOHN ROBIN 1967

Passengers and mail terminating at Thurso. Bovril was popular! SRPS

further afield, perhaps on the North Coast 500 route (500 miles by road), or, more traditionally, to the Orkney Islands. The North Coast 500 is promoted as 'the new scenic route showcasing fairytale castles, white sand beaches and historical ruins'. The Orkneys' principal appeal lies in its many pre-historic sites such as Skara Brae, Europe's best preserved Neolithic (Stone Age) human settlement.

To get to the Orkney Islands, public transport users take the train to Thurso and then hop on a bus or take a taxi for the 2-mile ride to the port of Scrabster, where NorthLink Ferries sails two or three times a day to Stromness, a westerly port on Mainland Orkney. Ferries also run to Orkney from two ports further east: Gills Bay to St Margaret's Hope (Pentland Ferries), or John O'Groats Ferries to Burwick on South Ronaldsay.

Final Destination: Wick

Back on the Far North train 'reversing' through Georgemas Junction towards Wick, there are likely to be quite a few empty seats. According to the Office of Rail and Road, Wick station had 18,000 passenger 'entries and exits' in 2017/18, against 30,000 for Thurso. The branch from Georgemas travels across unremarkable rural land along the valley of the River Wick, which is also used by two roads: the A882 and the B874.

Wick (with a population of 7,000) serves as a market and administrative town for the extensive agricultural area of Caithness, although it was once described as the 'herring capital' of Europe. Its name derives from 'vik', the Norse for 'bay', as does 'vik-ing': there are several villages in Norway called Vik. The River Wick meets the North Sea in a deep bay here; to the south of the bay is the suburb of Pulteneytown, originally a fishing community planned by Thomas Telford for the British Fisheries Society in 1786. Old Pulteney is a whisky distillery open to the public, and Pulteney-

Famous signpost at John O'Groats showing the distances (in kilometres) to various cities and to Land's End (1,018km) at the other end of Great Britain. ISTOCK.COM/CLAUDELUX

town also has the Wick Heritage Centre, a local museum.

Outside Wick, the No. 77 bus (at the time of writing there are three departures daily, Monday to Friday only) offers a twenty-nine-minute run along the coast to John O'Groats, for those interested in reaching the northernmost village on mainland Britain, 876 miles from Land's End, Cornwall. (It may be of interest here that in their YouTube site and book of 2017 *All The Stations*, Vicki Pipe and Geoff Marshall treated Wick station as their very last port of call, having started their marathon rail journey through all 2,563 mainland British rail stations at Penzance, Cornwall.)

Lost Lines in the North of Scotland

The Black Isle Line

The 'Black Isle Line' ran eastward from Muir of Ord, two stops south of Dingwall on the main Highland Railway line from Inverness, to the small town of Fortrose on the so-called Black Isle. (Officially it was the Fortrose branch of Highland Railway.) The intervening stops, all serving tiny communities, were at Redcastle, Allangrange, Munlochy and Avoch. Never profitable, it closed to passengers in 1951 (and freight in 1960, after which the track was lifted: the most substantial evidence of the line having existed is the station building at Redcastle, refurbished as the Nansen Highland youth training centre).

Although long gone, the story of the Black Isle Line was fascinating because it encapsulated some of the 'mania' that infected railways in the nineteenth century. Tactical manoeuvres between rival railway companies could be more akin to a military campaign than a plan for public transport. The rivals in this case were Highland Railway and Great North of Scotland (GNOS), which shared lines across Grampian but were often at loggerheads. In 1889, daring to step outside its Grampian territory, GNOS applied to Parliament to build a line from Fortrose to Muir of Ord, giving it a chance to reach Inverness using the Highland Line.

Highland parried this thrust with a Bill to create its own line from Muir of Ord to Rosemarkie (just beyond Fortrose), where passengers would take a ferry across the Moray Firth to the heart of GNOS's Grampian territory at Ardersier. Highland's Bill won the day and GNOS withdrew, but instead applied for running powers on the Aberdeen–Inverness line that the companies shared. Highland countered with a controversial proposal that the two enemies should merge, a suggestion immediately rejected by GNOS. Highland duly completed its Black Isle Line, but only as far as Fortrose. A second Black Isle Line, authorized in 1902, would have run from Conon Bridge along the north of the peninsula to Cromarty. By 1914, 6 miles of light railway track had been laid, but World War I ended this aspiration.

Further north, with a direct impact on the even-

LIGHT RAILWAYS IN THE HIGHLANDS

'Light' railways were an official category under the Light Railways Act (1896), an early instance of 'deregulation', in which lines could be built with a less onerous burden of safety rulings, and without the expense of submitting a Bill to Parliament. Many were built across Britain (under Light Railway Orders), but with a 25mph speed limit they provided no real competition to road traffic after the 1930s.

In the Highlands, the underlying economics of building only light railways were partly due to terrain. For the Wick–Lybster line, the hills reach the coast along the route, making for steep gradients (tunnel costs would be prohibitive), and plentiful level crossings were needed for the line to cross country roads.

In addition to Wick & Lybster, Dornoch Light, and Cromarty & Dingwall (never opened), Scottish light railways were built connecting Fraserburgh & St Combs (see Chapter 3), Leadhills & Wanlockhead (South Lanarkshire, with heritage service), Bankfoot (Perthshire), Campbeltown & Machrihanish (Argyll), Carmyllie (Angus), Lauder (Berwickshire) and Maidens & Dunure (Ayrshire).

tual Far North Line, were two branch lines (light railways), which succumbed to closure. As described above in this chapter, the railway line loops inland (to Lairg) around the Dornoch Firth, although a modern road bridge crosses it to reach the town of Dornoch. Between 1902 and 1960, a light railway set off from The Mound (south of Golspie) to serve Dornoch: a neatly laid out, former royal burgh with two championship golf courses, an ancient cathedral and good hotels. (Dornoch made global news in the year 2000 when the singer Madonna had her son Rocco christened in the cathedral, prior to marrying film director Guy Ritchie close to Dornoch at Skibo Castle, once the home of Scots-born philanthropist, Andrew Carnegie.)

Wick & Lybster

Closed down even earlier (in 1944) was another light railway branching from the Far North, from the terminus at Wick to Lybster, 14 miles down the North Sea coast. In contrast to the line serving picturesque Dornoch, Wick & Lybster was primarily intended for freight, particularly fish. The old ticket office at Lybster remains in use as the clubhouse of Lybster Golf Club, which uses a picture of a steam locomotive in the club logo.

Services on the Far North Line

In 2019 (19 May–14 December), ScotRail operated the following Far North services in their North Highlands timetable:

- Inverness to Thurso and Wick, Mon.–Sat.: Four daily departures between 7.00 and 18.31. Sun.: One daily service at 17.54 (arrive Wick 22.17)
- Thurso/Wick to Inverness, Mon.–Sat.: Four daily departures between 6.18 (Wick, 6.50 from Thurso) and 16.00 (Wick, 16.32 from Thurso). Sun.: One service, Wick 11.58, Thurso 12.30

Sources for Far North Line

(*See also* Sources, the chapter for general sources.)

Fenwick, K. and Sinclair N. T., *Lost Stations on the Far North Line: The Impact of the Railway Closures North of Inverness in 1960* (Highland Railway Society 2010)

Kernahan, J., *The Black Isle Railway* (Highland Railway Society 2013)

McConnell, D., *Rails to Wick & Thurso* (Dornoch 1989)

Price, D., *The Kyle of Lochalsh and Far North Lines* (Amberley 2018)

Spaven, D., *Highland Survivor: The Story of the Far North Line* (Kessock Books 2016)

Thomas, J. and Turnock, D., *A Regional History of the Railways of Great Britain Vol 15: The North of Scotland* (David & Charles 1989)

Internet (www.)
Friends of the Far North Line
(fofnl.org.uk)

Network Rail
(networkrail.co.uk) – page about Far North

Railscot.co.uk – primary resource for Scottish railway information

ScotRail
(ScotRail.co.uk) – official website of Abellio franchise

scot-rail
(scot-rail.co.uk) – 'Scotland's online rail enthusiast community'

CHAPTER 6

Railway Romance: the West Highland Line

One of the last truly romantic experiences left on the mainline railway system in Britain.

The Scotsman, 24 April 2018

The word 'romantic' is often used loosely, but it has two meanings of relevance to railways in the Scottish Highlands. First, it is used to denote much of European culture in the late nineteenth century, in poetry, prose, music, painting and even architecture. And second, 'romantic' reflects the dream-like quality of early investment in the West Highland Line, with the many challenges that it presented.

In the former sense, Romanticism was, ironically, a rejection of the very values represented by the railway boom: modernization of transport (replacing the horse), human technological progress, and above all, industry and its dirty, mass-producing factories. This progress was symbolized, in Scotland, by the rapidly expanding city of Glasgow, about which there was little of the romantic by the late nineteenth century.

Glasgow had risen rapidly to become the powerhouse of Scotland's industry: the Second City of Empire. The broader Strathclyde region was famed for shipbuilding, coal-mining, textiles and, appropriately, for the manufacture of steam locomotives and other rolling stock. North British Locomotive Company was the largest loco maker in Europe by 1903, after a series of mergers. Also making locos in Springburn were St Rollox (owned by Caledonian Railway) and Cowlairs (North British Railway, separately from the North British Loco. Co., which eventually liquidated in 1962). It was announced in 2019 that Gemini Rail Services would close the last remaining loco facility, Springburn Works, in 2020.

A Breath of Fresh Air

Glasgow was providing employment for displaced Highlanders and Irish immigrants, but it was also a city of growing pollution, poverty, malnourishment, disease and social unrest. So to depart for the Highlands by railway on the West Highland Line was, and still is, to breathe in the fresh air.

In the decades after the British railway 'mania' of the 1840s, the romantic vision of a railway running across uncharted territory through the ancient region of Lochaber had been no more than a dream. To begin with, the North British (founded 1844) and the Caledonian were competing for projects in busier areas of the Central Belt and northern England (for example, Glasgow to Carlisle). By 1858, trains from Glasgow had reached Helensburgh – the starting point of the West Highland – but the west coast further north had to wait until 1880 to be

West Highland Line between Tyndrum and Bridge of Orchy, looking to Beinn Odhar.

reached by rail (Callander & Oban: *see* Chapter 7, Reaching the West Coast).

By the early 1880s, the plight of highlands-and-islands small-scale farmers (the crofters) was attracting British government sympathy in the wake of the brutal Clearances and potato famines of the mid-century. National sympathy, enshrined in the Crofters Acts, strengthened the idea of improving transport in these remote regions of Britain.

In 1883, a new company was formed called the Glasgow & North Western Railway using a £300,000 British government grant – but the private funding came from North British, which would implement the West Highland Line. There were already lines running north from Glasgow (to Helensburgh, on the west coast, and Balloch, at the foot of Loch Lomond) established in the 1850s, but Glasgow & North Western proposed an ambitious, brand new line heading for the eastern shore of Loch Lomond, passing through suburbs and villages such as Milngavie,

Strathblane, Drymen and Balmaha. Thereafter, that line would have tracked today's West Highland, through Crianlarich, Tyndrum and Rannoch Moor, but it would also have continued through the Great Glen to reach Inverness.

The existing force in Inverness, Highland Railway, successfully opposed the Glasgow & North Western Bill in Parliament, and in its place a Bill was introduced that, with some alterations, came to fruition as the West Highland Line, as it is known today.

Expedition Across Rannoch Moor

Several unromantic business deals preceded the eventual launch of a West Highland line in 1894. But with actual funding – rather than pipedreams – in place by 1888, a group of professionals surveyed the moorland that the line would have to cross, on an exploration that would become the stuff of Scottish railway legend, if not romance.

The group of professional gentlemen who, in their smart office suits, took on the challenge of surveying the intimidating, soggy plateau of Rannoch Moor, set off from their Spean Bridge hotel in the depths of winter on 29 January 1889. The intrepid

group spent a month slogging 40 miles across the moor, passing the nights in remote lodges, cottages and simple 'bothies' (rural Highland huts), finally digging their way through snowdrifts in blizzard conditions to reach the town of Tyndrum (a station on the Callander–Oban line at that time).

The team of explorers comprised engineers Charles Forman, James Bulloch and J.E. Harrison of Forman & McCall; two factors – property managers – of estates on which the railway would be built; N.B. MacKenzie, a solicitor; and Robert McAlpine, building contractor. The company, led by the redoubtable and energetic Charles Forman (1852–1901), would take on the task of building the West Highland northwards from Helensburgh, using a workforce of up to 5,000 men.

Robert McAlpine (1847–1934), later Sir Robert (and also nicknamed 'concrete Bob'), would be responsible for building the Fort William to Mallaig extension of the West Highland, including the famous Glenfinnan Viaduct. His firm started in 1869 and was involved in building housing, factories, harbours and railway lines including the Glasgow Subway. (Today, Sir Robert McAlpine is the enduring name of a large private building and civil engineering company, with its HQ in England.)

Rannoch Moor: 'Glasgow–Fort William train lost in the vastness of the moor' (taken during 'fine weather in mid-May').
NORMAN MCNAB

The terrain over which a western line would have to travel presented much more formidable obstacles than the east of Scotland's relatively low-lying, continuous coast. The fjord-like nature of the west coast, together with the moor and mountain terrain, had always contributed to isolation for the western highlands and islands. Hence the relatively late arrival of the West Highland Line, which was finally opened for business on 7 August 1894.

The West Highland: Station by Station

A Historic Journey from Helensburgh to Fort William

Look out of the window – you'll travel through a daunting landscape of mountains, steep-sided lochs, and heather moors. Keep an eye out for red deer, silhouetted on a skyline or half-hidden in the heather. You'll pass some of the smallest, remotest stations on the network – a few buildings, and nothing more for miles around. And you'll be glad you've come by train, passing through country where no roads were ever built.

ScotRail website 2019

Officially, ScotRail's West Highland service sets off from Queen Street station in the centre of Glasgow, but this chapter will concentrate on the line starting further north, from Helensburgh Upper. (Chapter 4 detailed Queen Street and the role of Glasgow in Scottish rail.) Geographically, the line spends most of its time in the council area of Argyll & Bute before briefly running across the western edge of the Stirling council area at Crianlarich and Tyndrum. It then divides, with one branch continuing to Fort William – in the Highland council area – and the other heading west to Oban (back into Argyll & Bute). From Fort William, a separate branch travels west to the coast at Mallaig. The branches to Oban and Mallaig are described in Chapter 7, 'Reaching the West Coast'.

Before reaching Helensburgh, the West Highland makes its way through the western suburbs of

Glasgow and urban West Dunbartonshire, passing through the historic shipbuilding towns of Clydebank and Dumbarton. Along the River Clyde estuary, trains cross the eastern end of the historic Forth & Clyde Canal, whose use, like that of the Caledonian Canal further north, was curtailed by the arrival of rail in the early nineteenth century.

At Dumbarton (population 20,000), the West Highland meets the North Clyde Line for trains to Balloch, on Loch Lomond, while trains on the West Highland fork off along the riverbank of the Clyde on a fifteen-minute run to reach Helensburgh, the historic starting point of the West Highland (and of the Highland Boundary Fault: Helensburgh lies on the western end of the Highland Boundary Fault, the geological feature used in physical geography to divide Scotland's Highlands from its Lowlands; its north-easterly undergound passage reaches the east coast at Stonehaven, 130 miles away on the East Coast railway line).

Helensburgh

A prosperous town of 15,600 people, many of them commuters to Glasgow, Helensburgh was developed from an earlier village by the local laird, James Colquhoun, who renamed it after his wife, Helen. The elegant Georgian and, later, Victorian townhouses were settled by wealthy and famous individuals, including Henry Bell, the paddle steamer pioneer; John Logie Baird, a pioneer of television; and publisher Walter Blackie, who commissioned the famous Hill House (by Charles Rennie Mackintosh) to be built as his Helensburgh residence.

Helensburgh Upper and Craigendoran
The West Highland station, Helensburgh Upper, is a five-minute walk from Hill House within a sedate suburb, whereas the original railway (and river traffic) action took place closer to the town centre, a fifteen-minute walk downhill from Helensburgh Upper. A riverside station (just 'Helensburgh') had opened on the Glasgow, Dumbarton & Helensburgh Line in 1858, and for the next twenty years, rail traffic – for goods and passengers – was integrated with river traffic at Helensburgh pier. In 1882, North

Class 156493 departing for Glasgow from the single-platform station at Helensburgh Upper. Uniquely on West Highland, access to the platform is by walkway down from the road, not the subway (Railscot).

Old Craigendoran station with its three platforms and covered pier. SRPS

Sunset at derelict Craigendoran pier, once a hive of commercial and transport activity.

British Railway – also a steamship operator – moved its operations out of town to Craigendoran, a mile up the Clyde. Local businesses and politicians had objected to building a bigger pier within Helensburgh, and Craigendoran became a busy transport hub right up to the 1960s.

At its opening in 1894, the West Highland started at Craigendoran Upper station and avoided Helensburgh town centre, climbing steeply through residential streets – as it does today – to Helensburgh Upper. Today, Craigendoran's old pier is a sad sight.

Garelochhead

Despite Helensburgh's appeal, the majority of West Highland passengers stay seated for the next half hour as the line leaves the River Clyde behind to travel along the shore of a sea loch with an unusual 'reverse' name: Gare Loch, rather than Loch Gare; it reaches the head of the loch at the precisely named

Garelochhead station, the first station on the West Highland proper. The coastal run from Helensburgh to Garelochhead affords views across to the Rosneath peninsula, where a grand castle (demolished in 1961) was once home to Princess Louise, Queen Victoria's sixth child. (Louise had married the Marquis of Argyll, later the Duke of Argyll and Chief of Clan Campbell; the ducal estate of Argyll is one of the largest in Scotland.)

The head of the loch is today most famous (or infamous) as the location of 'Faslane' – officially, Her Majesty's Naval Base Clyde – where the Submarine Service is based, including the nuclear-equipped Tridents. Much of the land north of Garelochhead is also reserved by the Ministry of Defence for training and storing munitions. Leaving Garelochhead, the train crosses an isthmus between Gare Loch and Loch Long, beside which the line runs quietly for 10 miles to the next station.

Glen Douglas

As on all Highland railways, the West Highland passes through many former stations or halts; on the run from Helensburgh, these included Rhu (or Row), Shandon, Whistlefield (serving the lochside village of Portincaple) and Glen Douglas. The later station had a convoluted railway history: it was called a 'siding' from 1895 to 1926, then a platform to 1942, when it was used by school children of railway staff undergoing training here, and thereafter simply as 'Glen Douglas'; it was a private station to 1964, when it closed.

The Glen Douglas name was commemorated in a William Reid steam locomotive now preserved at the Riverside Museum of Transport in Glasgow.

Arrochar & Tarbet

Past Glen Douglas, the line runs behind Ardmay House, nowadays a children's outdoor education centre, and skirts the lochside village of Arrochar at the head of Loch Long. The stop for Arrochar is a mile further on at the start of the village of Tarbet, hence the station name of Arrochar & Tarbet. A 'tarbet' is an isthmus between lakes – there are several in the Scottish gazetteer – but it derives from the Gaelic for 'drag boat', which refers to the ancient practice of dragging ships across dry land between lakes or rivers.

Some passengers will board or alight at Arrochar & Tarbet because of its connections by rail and road. The A83 passes through here as a crucial east-west connection across the hills known as the Arrochar

'Glen Douglas' (Riverside Museum of Transport, Glasgow). Built at the Cowlairs Works in 1913 for North British Railway as NBR no. 256, later LNER iClass D34 as engine 9256 ('Glen' class), then BR 62469.

Alps to Loch Fyne, and the village also connects to the road from Glasgow, the A82, which winds all the way up the west shore of Loch Lomond. (Although this is the main route north by road, building a railway along this shore was never seriously contemplated, it would seem.)

At the Ballyhennan burial ground, close to Arrochar & Tarbet station, there is a memorial to those who worked on the railway, erected in 1994 on the centenary of the line opening. The Arrochar, Tarbet & Ardlui Heritage Group have documented their area's history in detail, the website (arrocharheritage.com) including a page on the building of the West Highland, with interesting reminiscences about the 'navvies' (*see* panel).

From Arrochar & Tarbet, the railway crosses the Tarbet or 'isthmus' between Loch Long and the next lochside run, this time along the famous Loch Lomond, albeit elevated above the loch to avoid the busy A82 roadway. At the village of Inveruglas, the line runs above and behind the elegant building housing the Loch Sloy hydroelectric power station; passengers have a view up the line of four steel pipes connecting the station to the valve house on the hill. (Loch Sloy is one of over ninety major hydroelectric schemes across Scotland: *see* description in Chapter 7, Falls of Cruachan on the Oban line).

Ardlui

The next station, at Ardlui, offers a hotel, a holiday park, a marina and a seasonal ferry across Loch Lomond for hikers on the West Highland Way, which runs up the east side of the loch. Loch Lomond is today a recreational facility for the city of Glasgow, but visitors also know it for the song *The Bonnie Banks o' Loch Lomond*, with its famous chorus about 'taking the high road'. Loch Lomond is the best known loch passed by a railway, but the Highland lines encounter many others (*see* panel.) On a clear day the summit of Ben Lomond (3,196ft) can be seen on the east side of the loch.

BUILDING THE HIGHLAND RAILWAYS: THE NAVVIES

The term 'navvy' derived from the so-called navigators who dug the eighteenth-century canals (or navigations), some of whom moved on to excavating the permanent ways.

Arrocharheritage.com has a page on the building of the West Highland, with interesting reminiscences about the navvies. Some 5,000 navvies were housed and fed in camps at Helensburgh, Arrochar, Ardlui and Crianlarich, where nurses and medicines were available. But the records show that thirty-seven of them died in this area, ranging in age from eighteen to sixty-eight, the vast majority single men such as Peter Murphy, aged thirty, who died after 'an explosion at Creaganardain'.

Other research by Arrochar Heritage concludes that:

- 'Working conditions were appalling, with little or no shelter….the men would have been wet to the bone for much of the time'
- Church ministers set up libraries for the workers: 'this helped to keep the men off the drink'
- 'The workers didn't mix very much with the local communities. The men were a mix of Highlanders, Irishmen, Poles…'
- 'Some railwaymen probably went to the village dances at the Arrochar'
- 'The Irish navvies didn't stay long due to the remoteness and conditions, and went down to England where there was more social life'

Loch Lomond at Inveruglas, showing a cruiser (foreground) and Loch Sloy hydro-electric power station (the West Highland Line passes above).

LOCHS OF THE HIGHLANDS

The map of Scotland shows few lochs on the east of the country, while the west coast is peppered with both sea lochs – fjords flowing into the Atlantic – and land-locked, freshwater lochs. This geographical feature, combined with mountainous terrain in the west, was a factor in the East Coast Line developing much earlier than the West Highland Line.

The Highlands have dozens of large lochs, but the most notable ones encountered on the West Highland route northwards are the following (with their length in miles):

- Gare Loch (6 miles), a sea loch emptying into the River Clyde estuary
- Loch Long (20 miles), which stretches from Arrochar southwards into the Clyde
- Loch Lomond (22 miles), the largest loch in Scotland by surface area, and famous for its song, The Bonnie Banks o' Loch Lomond
- Loch Treig (5 miles), converted into a reservoir
- Loch Linnhe (31 miles), the sea loch at Fort William
- Loch Eil (6 miles), Loch Shiel and others (Mallaig branch)
- Loch Awe (25 miles), the longest but narrowest loch in Scotland, on the Oban line

Other notable Highland lochs are Loch Ness, which contains the largest volume of water, and Loch Morar (seen from the line to Mallaig), which is the deepest, at 1,107ft.

The number of lochs is a result of the wet climate and mountainous terrain (the valleys are filled by water), but their depth is because they were hollowed out by glaciers during the Ice Age. Smaller lochs (there are many scattered across Rannoch Moor) are called 'lochans'.

Crianlarich 'looking south', with some potential for mischief! SRPS

By Ardlui, Loch Lomond has tapered to a narrow stretch of water giving way northwards to the river, which feeds the lake from Glen Falloch. The Falls of Falloch, sometimes a spectacular cascade, can be glimpsed on the other side of the glen. The Drovers Inn is another striking sight: nowadays a characterful hotel, pub and restaurant, the inn was built in 1705 to service clansmen 'droving' (driving) their cattle to lowland markets, or trysts.

Crianlarich

Just under two hours from Glasgow, the West Highland train pulls into Crianlarich, where it will divide for the branches to Fort William or Oban. In Gaelic, Crianlarich means 'low pass', but a glance at a map shows that the town is a significant junction, not just for rail but also for road, and in previous times, for drovers and soldiers. The rail line arrives with the A82 from Glasgow to meet the A85 from the east, and five long-distance bus routes pass through Crianlarich.

Crianlarich had two stations when the West Highland opened in 1894, the first having been built lower in the town by Callander & Oban in 1873 (*see* 'Lost Lines in the West Highlands', later in this chapter). The present station was once called Crianlarich Upper, but reverted to just Crianlarich with the closure of Callander & Oban in 1965. (The line from Crianlarich to Oban remains; it was the Callander–Crianlarich stretch that closed.) Sidings at the station are used for storing permanent way materials.

The Two Tyndrums

The West Highland divides at Crianlarich, and passengers for either Oban or Fort William have a few minutes to wait and can stretch their legs on the platform while the train divides. The front two carriages (of four) head west on the spur to Oban, while the rear carriages continue northwards for Rannoch Moor and Fort William; the lines run on opposite sides of the River Fillan. Both trains then pass through the village of Tyndrum, but the branch for Fort William calls at Upper Tyndrum (as does the Caledonian Sleeper), while the Oban branch

FAMOUS GLENS ON THE WEST HIGHLAND

The plentiful valleys known as glens or straths in Scotland are a feature of this mountainous, glaciated landscape with plentiful rainfall. The western Highlands get 118in of rain a year, as against 31in on the east coast, and 22in in London.

Highland glens are usually gently U-shaped rather than V-shaped, due to the action of glaciers in the Ice Age; the straths – mostly floodplain land – are even wider and shallower, which made it easier to build railways through them. The West Highland runs through Glen Falloch, Strath Fillan, Glen Spean and, on the way to Oban, Glen Lochy.

These passages through glens contribute to the picturesque journey, but the problem for building the West Highland railway northwards was not the gradients in the glens but their frequent occurrence running east–west to the sea. This interrupted north–south construction, necessitating pauses while bridges were built. (The east coast has fewer glens to cross, but two mighty estuaries necessitated building the Forth and Tay bridges.)

Glencoe is Scotland's most famous and most visited glen, its dramatic scenery used by numerous film crews over the years; it was also the site of the infamous massacre of 1692 involving the McDonald and Campbell clans. The steep gradients – Glencoe is geologically a relatively young valley – precluded the building of a railway through it: hence the detour over Rannoch Moor for Fort William.

Sadly, trains no longer run along the steep sides of Glen Ogle (once on the Callander–Oban line) but the railway viaduct – now a hiking and cycle path – remains as a spectacular reminder of a line that might have been saved.

Glen Ogle viaduct from the north, now on a cycling/ walking route, once a highlight of the Callander & Oban journey. JOHN ROBIN, 2010

stops at Tyndrum Lower. (It was just 'Tyndrum' when it opened in 1877 on the Oban line.)

The two Tyndrum stations are several minutes' walk from the centre of the village, the winding road up to Upper Tyndrum offering a steep challenge. This elevated position was necessary for the line to gain height steadily from the river valley (Strathfillan) up to the County March Summit (1,024ft) beyond Tyndrum.

Tyndrum itself is even smaller than Crianlarich by population (167 residents), but it is also a key transport hub and a natural place to break a journey. Like the railway lines, the roads split after Tyndrum, the A82 heading for Fort William and the A85 for the west coast and Oban.

Departing Upper Tyndrum is where, for many West Highland passengers, the romance of the journey truly begins. On board there is a perceptible intake of breath as the train enters Glen Orchy, where the vista from the train opens out magnificently into a mixture of mountain panoramas, commercial forestry and a summer parade through the valley of motorists, cyclists, hikers and campers. The railway line here is one of no fewer than six means of transport, old and new, through this valley: there were drove roads and military roads to which were added the railway and then the metalled road (A82); later came the hiking trail (West Highland Way), also used by mountain bikers.

Bridge of Orchy

Crossing the valley through which Allt Kinglas runs – 'allt' is Gaelic for a stream, or burn – forces the train to use the long, curved Horseshoe Viaduct (or 'curve'), which for many is a visual highlight of this journey. The viaduct is 576ft long over nine 60ft spans of latticed girders. The line then curves round the foot of Ben Dorain (3,524ft) to pause at Bridge of Orchy.

All Aboard! Bridge of Orchy Station

The fifteen-minute ride from Upper Tyndrum to Bridge of Orchy is one of the most scenic stretches on any Highland line: high mountains, deep valley,

streams, hikers on their trail and sheep grazing quietly.

The hamlet called Bridge of Orchy offers thirty-two bedrooms at the 4-star Bridge of Orchy Hotel, or budget accommodation at the station itself, where the West Highland Way Sleeper, occupying the main station buildings, offers bunkhouse accommodation for hikers (one mixed-gender 'dorm' of ten bunks).

Opened in 1894, Bridge of Orchy station is a typical Highland station with a crossing loop and an island platform, necessitating a pedestrian underpass to reach the platforms. The buildings were built in a classical Swiss chalet style, popular on Highland stations. There are sidings on the east side used for maintenance vehicles.

The best evidence of Bridge of Orchy being in hill-walking territory is provided by the rough concrete steps at the station's 'back', leading the walker straight to the hills of Ben an Dothaidh and Ben Dorain, or to regain the West Highland Way.

Rannoch Moor

Departing Bridge of Orchy, the train offers views west to Loch Tulla before diverging from the road route into open moorland, leaving behind the A82 with its coaches, campers and bikers. The road route snakes up westwards to the Black Mount viewpoint and on towards the famous valley of Glencoe, while the West Highland Line quietly sneaks eastwards and then north again into the true wilderness of Rannoch Moor.

> A wearier-looking desert man never saw.
>
> David Balfour, hero of *Kidnapped*
> by Robert Louis Stevenson

The moor is a 50 square mile, elevated plateau – mostly 1,000ft above sea level – which can be beautiful in the summer sunshine, when the mauve heather is in bloom, or as bleak as a moonscape when the mist descends. To the south and west lie the Glencoe Mountain Resort and the King's House Hotel complex (extended and reopened in 2019), but otherwise the whole area is designated for conservation and is a Site of Special Scientific Interest. In

Stairway at the rear exit of Bridge of Orchy station, leading immediately to a mountain path.

'Just south of Rannoch station on a February afternoon': the 12.21 from Glasgow (number 156447). NORMAN MCNAB

fact although roe deer and the occasional feral goat roam the moor, scientific interest comes mainly from the teeming but tiny wildlife and rare plant species that inhabit the peat bog and lochans (small lakes). Therefore little human activity intrudes on nature except for the railway line, and hikers on the West Highland Way.

Building a railway across the deep bog was impossible in a conventional way, so foundations had to be laid using ashes, earth, tree roots and brushwood, on which the railway line – like parts of the road – would 'float'.

In such a deserted landscape, stations are naturally few and far between: it takes the train eleven minutes to travel from Crianlarich to Tyndrum, then sixteen minutes to Bridge of Orchy, and

twenty-one minutes to the next stop, Rannoch Station. There was a private station and signal box at Gorton, demolished in 1964; it once had a school for eleven children in a carriage on the island platform.

Rannoch Station

Capturing the rugged romance of the West Highland, Rannoch station is a small outpost of civilization sitting at the eastern end of the B846, the only road crossing the moor other than the busy A82 to Glencoe. By road, it takes twenty minutes driving eastwards to the village of Kinloch Rannoch, and another forty-five minutes to the larger town of Pitlochry (a stop on the Highland Main Line). For a quick bite, a tearoom occupies the old waiting room on the island platform of Rannoch station, coupled

Approaching Corrour station: 'A view looking back from the track to Loch Ossian'. NORMAN MCNAB

with a small shop selling essentials for hikers and climbers.

For those planning to stop at Rannoch, remoteness is celebrated at The Moor of Rannoch 'restaurant with rooms' next to the station: 'With no TV/ radio /WiFi signal and almost non-existent mobile coverage, The Moor of Rannoch is the perfect antidote to the modern fast-paced world.'

Between trains there is a chance to explore the beach on lonely Loch Laidon.

Corrour

Next on the line, Corrour is an even more remote outpost than Rannoch, qualifying as one of the highest UK stations – 1,339ft above sea level – and 16 miles from the nearest road. Apart from a waiting room, the station itself has no staff or facilities for the rail passenger, but adjacent Station House offers a restaurant and three rooms (in the old signal box) as part of the Corrour estate (*see* panel).

In addition to the Corrour estate properties, there is Loch Ossian hostel (Scottish Youth Hostels Association, SYHA), which has 'eco-hostel' status, using its own local hydro-electricity and solar power and with 'composting toilets and a reed bed to soak away grey water'. For the first eighty-five years of its history as a primitive 'bothy' there were only cold showers to be had.

Modern technology has, however, intruded near Corrour in the shape of twenty-first-century location filming. The station appeared, satirically, in both of the raunchy *Trainspotting* movies (1996 and 2017, both starring Ewan McGregor and Robert Carlyle) and in *Harry Potter And The Deathly Hallows: Part 1*

CORROUR: HISTORY OF A HIGHLAND ESTATE

The land around Corrour station is a 65,000 acre estate controlled by a Trust since 2003. The Swedish family who acquired the land in 1995 were 'enchanted by the Scottish mountain landscape', noticing place names with Nordic origins.

From the fourteenth century, the land around Loch Treig was home to the Macdonalds of Keppoch, but the estate was developed by various owners from the late nineteenth to the mid-twentieth centuries, firstly for shooting (deer, grouse) and fishing (trout, salmon), then for forestry. Sir John Stirling Maxwell (1866–1956) bought the estate in 1892: a politician and philanthropist, he was influential in the development of the Forestry Commission, the National Trust for Scotland and the Scottish Youth Hostel Association.

Sir John built a fine hunting lodge with landscaped gardens at the eastern end of Loch Ossian; the lodge burned down in 1942 but has been rebuilt as an estate office and modern home. Cottages and bothies on the estate are holiday lets with activities including shooting, fishing and pony trekking. There is also accommodation in Station House and in the converted signal box on the station platform.

The Corrour estate website has information about the management of the estate, with good photographs and videos including unique bird's-eye views over the station and its buildings, and a train arriving (https://www.corrour.co.uk).

(2010), in which the Hogwarts Express was stopped and searched by Death Eaters on the Corrour–Rannoch stretch.

After Corrour, there is a quiet 5-mile run with views to the left of Loch Treig, which has the appearance of a typically elongated Highland loch. As another intrusion of modern technology into the ancient landscape, the original loch was converted in 1929 into a dammed reservoir to provide water for the Lochaber hydro-electric plant at Fort William.

Tulloch and Roy Bridge

From the northern end of Loch Treig, the line starts its descent from the moor into Glen Spean, where

Curving past the River Spean between Tulloch and Roybridge.
SRPS

the fast-flowing River Spean opens out westwards, passing two small stations: Tulloch, where the station buildings are now The Station Lodge hostel, with bunks for twenty-four people; and Roy Bridge, serving the small village known as Roybridge. Roy Bridge is now a single platform with a modern waiting shelter; in the buildings on the original second platform (demolished in 1966) there was a large waiting room that was used every other Sunday morning for Church of Scotland services. (On alternate Sundays, the minister conducted services at Rannoch station, according to *The Story of the West Highland*.)

Spean Bridge

River sports are possible on both the Spean and its tributary, the Roy, with ample accommodation at Spean Bridge (population 540), where in the station itself there is The Old Station restaurant and bar. To arrive at Spean Bridge, the railway line parallels the busy east–west A86 trunk road that runs for 30 miles past Loch Laggan before connecting to the A9 at Kingussie (a station on the Highland Main Line). The even busier A82 from Fort William (south) and Inverness (north) also converges on the hamlet of Spean Bridge, with its woollen mill outlet shop, hotel, coach stop and cafés. In fact Spean Bridge was the actual terminus of the Invergarry & Fort Augustus Line (1903–1946): *see* the section 'Lost Lines in the West Highlands', below in this chapter.

After Spean Bridge, the West Highland 'reverses' direction by heading south-west for the terminus at Fort William. As the town approaches alongside the A82, a variety of local businesses are signposted from the road: the Nevis Range Mountain Experience; Fort William Golf Club; Ben Nevis Distillery; the Lochaber aluminium smelter, originally with its own narrow-gauge spur; and the stadium for the town's shinty club, lying across Camanachd Crescent.

Fort William: Hub of the Western Highlands

The final destination chosen for the West Highland was, naturally enough, the largest town in this region of Scotland. It was originally known as 'Inverlochy', then renamed after King William III, who was installed as British king after the deposition of James II in 1688, part of an assertion of dominance by the monarchy in the potentially rebellious Highlands.

The Gaelic translation on the station signs retains another old town name: 'An Gearasdan', or The Garrison (at the mouth of River Lochy).

With a population of 10,500 today, Fort William is second only to Inverness (population 60,000)

Before 1975, arriving at Fort William offered welcoming views over Loch Linnhe; the station was then relocated inland. JOHN ROBIN 1965

among Highland settlements, so it is an important hub for the community, not least by hosting the region's main hospital. Although scarred by some of its twentieth-century architecture, the town offers plenty of local employment and does not suffer a shortage of visitor accommodation: the booking.com website alone offers a choice of fifty-five hotels, 'B&B' or hostels ranging from the exclusive Inverlochy Castle to backpacker hostels.

Fort William station lost its original stone buildings in 1975 when they were replaced by a practical, if brutal, station next to a Morrisons superstore, large car park and bus terminal. Arriving passengers may, however, be treated to the sight of steam from *The Jacobite* – either a Black 5 or a K1 – waiting by platform 1. (The Jacobite heritage service is covered in Chapter 7: Reaching the West Coast.)

Alighting at Fort William from the West Highland (or the Caledonian Sleeper), passengers may variously be transferring to bus connections at the station, hiking onwards to their accommodation for the night, or exploring the town's High Street, which has half-a-mile of shops, bars and restaurants geared to a mixture of locals and visitors. At the far end of the High Street is an outdoor seating area with a sculpture of a seated man rubbing his feet – the Sore Feet statue – which marks the end of the 96-mile West Highland Way hiking trail from Glasgow.

Lost Lines in the West Highlands

The Callander & Oban line (C&O) mentioned above (at Crianlarich) could be covered in one of several 'journey' chapters of this book, because it really started in central Scotland and, almost uniquely, ran east–west rather than north–south through the Highlands.

Dunblane, Doune & Callander

Regarding Oban, there was an impetus to connect

The disused railway bridge near St Fillans, formerly on Callander & Oban, but closed under Beeching; it is now part of a hiking/cycling trail.

the western coast, which will be explored in Chapter 7 (Reaching the West Coast), but also an impetus to build westwards from the central counties of Perthshire and Stirlingshire, which had seen a proliferation of railway lines in the mid-nineteenth century (especially connecting Perth and Stirling). Opened in 1858, Dunblane, Doune & Callander connected two small but significant towns. Dunblane remains important as a terminus on ScotRail's 'central' services (Glasgow or Edinburgh to Dunblane via Stirling have their own timetable) and has direct onward services to Perth, Inverness or Dundee.

Callander lost its railway in 1965, although it was (and still is) an important calling point for tourists, and had been enjoying a tourism boom in the 1950s and 1960s, prior to losing its station. Doune is a small village between the two main stops, propelled to prominence recently by the filming of *Outlander* at its castle (and before that, of *Monty Python and the Holy Grail*).

The dream of extending a line from Callander westwards brought engineering challenges and the usual problem of running a line through a lightly populated region. Typically for a Highland line, however, the arrival of the railway brought economic and population growth to villages such as Strathyre, reached by the C&O line along Loch Lubnaig. After a stop at Lochearnhead (which would, much later, be served by another line along Loch Earn to Comrie) came the challenge of building through beautiful Glen Ogle, with a station serving Killin, and finally through Glen Dochart to Crianlarich. The story of reaching Oban from Crianlarich is taken up in Chapter 7, but in total the line(s) from Dunblane through to Oban took fourteen years to complete (1866–80), an unusually long time for the usually frenetic railway business of the nineteenth century.

Invergarry & Fort Augustus

Another lost line fraught with problems of development was called Invergarry & Fort Augustus (the Act was obtained in 1896), although it started at Spean Bridge station (on the West Highland).

Wending its way through farmland and along the Great Glen lochsides, only a few stops were built – at Gairlochy, Invergloy, Invergarry and Aberchalder, before reaching Fort Augustus at the foot of Loch Ness. Never profitable, the line closed to passengers in 1933 (and to freight in 1946). Little remains of the line, but Invergarry Station Museum has replaced a section of standard-gauge track with a 1947 diesel shunter, and a trolley provides rides.

Services on the West Highland

In 2019, ScotRail operated the following West Highlands services (timetable 20 May–8 December):

- Glasgow Queen Street to Oban or Fort William. Mon.–Sat.: Six daily (division at Crianlarich). Sun.: Four daily. Some departures summer only
- Fort William to Mallaig. Mon.–Sat.: Four daily. Sun.: Three daily

West Coast Railways (referred to in the ScotRail timetable as The Jacobite Steam Train) operated daily morning and afternoon services between Fort William and Mallaig (for example, 10.15 dep. Fort William arr. Mallaig 12.25, return 14.10–16.00 ('morning') or 18.38–20.31 ('afternoon')

Caledonian Sleeper operated sleeper services (room or seat, reservations only) from London Euston at 21.15 Mon.–Fri. (Sun. 21.00) via Edinburgh (4.50 pick-up only), Glasgow (5.48 pick-up only), arriving Fort William at 9.57

Sources for the West Highland

(*See also* the Sources chapter for general sources.)

The History of the Railways of the Scottish Highlands (series 1977–1990):
    Originally published by David & Charles, now from House of Lochar, Isle of Colonsay
    1. Thomas, J., *The West Highland Railway*

Northern Books from Famedram Publishers:
The Rannoch Line 1983
The Story of the West Highland: The 1940s LNER Guide 2001 (reprint)
Rails Across Rannoch 2013

McGregor, J., *The West Highland Line: Great Railway Journeys Through Time* (Amberley 2013)

Thomas, J. and Turnock, D., *A Regional History of the Railways of Great Britain Vol 15: The North of Scotland* (David & Charles 1989)

Victorian Travel on the West Highland Line: By Mountain, Moor and Loch in 1894 (House of Lochar 2002)

Internet (www.)
Arrochar, Tarbet and Ardlui Heritage (arrocharheritage.com)

Friends of the West Highland Lines (westhighlandline.org.uk)

Network Rail (networkrail.co.uk) – page about West Highland

Railscot.co.uk – primary resource for Scottish railway information

ScotRail (ScotRail.co.uk) – official website of Abellio franchise

scot-rail (scot-rail.co.uk) – 'Scotland's online rail enthusiast community'

West Highland Community Rail Partnership (westhighlandcrp.com)

CHAPTER 7

Reaching the West Coast: Oban, Mallaig and Kyle of Lochalsh

David Spaven's comprehensive coverage of Scottish railway maps through history – *The Railway Atlas of Scotland* (Birlinn, 2015) – shows that once the obvious priorities of connecting Glasgow, Edinburgh and English cities had been achieved, the main thrust within Scotland was from south to north. That is, the investment potential lay in building lines northwards, as far as was practicable, from the Central Belt to the settlements at Aberdeen, Inverness and Fort William.

By the end of the 1860s, absorptions and mergers had collapsed a dozen small Highland operators into three large groups – Highland, Great North of Scotland and Caledonian – and rail routes were well established from the south to Aberdeen and Inverness, with much of the eventual Far North Line completed. In the 1870s the impetus was to take trains towards the west coast of Scotland, although it would take another twenty years for the long West Highland Line to be completed, finally connecting Glasgow to the important hub at Fort William.

This chapter looks at the development of three east–west railway lines: the line from Inverness via Dingwall to Kyle of Lochalsh (not fully completed until 1897), and two branches from the West Highland: Crianlarich to Oban (reached in 1880) and Fort William to Mallaig (1901).

First and Foremost: The Fish

Seafood had always been a major component of the Scottish diet, but it was the British Fisheries Society (its full name The British Society for Extending the Fisheries and Improving the Sea Coasts), founded by Act of Parliament in 1786, that led to a more industrial approach to fishing based in purpose-built coastal towns. In the boom times for sea fishing up to a century ago, 'silver darlings' was the nickname given to the billions of herring (*Clupea harengus*) that supported Scottish fishing. Herring fishing reached a peak just before World War I when over 2.5 million barrels were packed for export by thousands of 'herring lassies'.

The railways had made their contribution after 1850 by speeding up the journey made by fresh or frozen fish from Highland harbours to markets in the cities of the south. The early use of railways for transporting fish and farm produce echoed their primary use, even earlier, for freighting coal and iron ore in the south of Scotland.

The decline of fishing is poignantly summed up in the folk song, 'Fareweel tae the haven', written for The McCalmans by Davy Steele:

I'm leaving the fishin', the life I have known
The battle with nature that nobody won

For the fish stocks are dwindlin' and the shoals hard
to find

I'm leaving the fishin', I've made up my mind

The 'dwindlin'' fish stocks was one reason for the decline of sea fishing, but changes in eating habits – there was more meat to buy at a reasonable price – and foreign competition across European seas also contributed to the decline.

Transporting fish and farm produce was a primary motive for building railways within the Highlands and to the coasts, but the lines developed new roles in the twentieth century. Today they are useful for local residents (especially rural school children), but their main function, increasing with every passing year, is to furnish pleasant and convenient transits for tourists and leisure travellers.

From Steamers to Ferries, and 'Calmac'

It was important for railways to reach the west coast to pick up passengers who travelled up the coast from Glasgow on steamers that were sometimes owned by the railway companies. But the ports had another obvious attraction: reaching the many offshore islands that make up the 'Highlands and Islands' of northern Scotland, and which appeal to the roving tourist.

Once Oban, Mallaig and Kyle of Lochalsh were connected to the rail network, ferries set sail from them to the islands, with Oban promoting itself as the 'gateway to the isles', while the Fort William to Mallaig route is known as the 'road to the isles'. Kyle of Lochalsh remains an important coastal terminus for rail, although its ferry service was usurped by the bridge to the Isle of Skye, completed in 1995.

Most west coast ferries are operated by 'CalMac', shorthand for Caledonian MacBrayne. As its nickname suggests, CalMac was born from a corporate merger: the Caledonian Steam Packet Company and David MacBrayne Ltd (founded in 1851) came together into CalMac in 1973. The 'steam packet' shipping company had taken the name of its railway parent (Caledonian Railway), which, like other railway companies of the nineteenth century, tried to offer their customers a combination of train, ferry or autobus whenever necessary.

The railway Grouping of 1923 brought together the shipping fleets owned by Caledonian and Glasgow & South West, while nationalization in 1948 brought in the former North British Railway fleet. CalMac is controlled by the Scottish government and has a virtual monopoly on scheduled services

Busy Oban. Foreground: CalMac ferry and railway station. Background: promenade and town centre with McCaig's Tower above.'
NORMAN MCNAB

to the Western Isles. The thirty-three vessels sail on fifty routes, carrying over five million passengers and 80,000 commercial vehicles annually.

Journeys to the Coast (1): Crianlarich to Oban

The story of the complete Callander & Oban Line was told in Chapter 6 (West Highland Line), where it was treated as a 'lost line', but the western half of the line remains, connecting Crianlarich with the coast at Oban. At Crianlarich, trains divide to head either north via Tyndrum to Rannoch Moor and Fort William, or westwards – also through Tyndrum – towards Oban. Technically, both journeys are part of today's West Highland Line.

The branch to Oban takes just over an hour, as against the circuitous ninety-minute run to Fort William. The first part of the journey is bucolic, perhaps less spectacular than crossing Rannoch Moor, but along the way are several iconic remind-ers of Scotland's past history, as well as some modern tourist destinations: the dramatic ruins of Kilchurn Castle; the beauty of St Conan's Kirk; and the towering Ben Cruachan with its underground power station.

The Callander & Oban took ten years to complete from 1870 while funding was located for each stretch, building steadily westwards from Callander to Crianlarich, and then on to Tyndrum by 1873. Later on, the West Highland (as it was known then) required its own station on the hillside above Tyndrum, so Tyndrum Upper was created, leaving the C&O station as Lower Tyndrum. Parlia-mentary approval had to be gained to continue the line beyond Tyndrum, in which Caledonian Rail-way (which worked the line) was instrumental, as a major investor in the line.

Dalmally

From Tyndrum Lower, trains head west alongside the River Lochy, parallel to the A85 main road,

Dalmally station en route to Oban. The signal box (foreground) is disused, but the station building is occupied by craft studio and 'quirky' accommodation.

CASTLES ON THE HIGHLAND WEST COAST

Many ruined fortresses are visible on Scotland's west coast as a reminder of how the land was controlled from the sea during the stormy days of invasions from Ireland or by the Norse, and there were constant struggles between the MacDonalds (Lords of the Isles) and the powerful Campbell clan.

Kilchurn Castle, seen from the Oban line, was a Campbell stronghold for two centuries until it was struck by lightning in 1760 and abandoned. In this period, the crushing of the mid-century Jacobite Rebellions led to many Highland castles being purposely destroyed or abandoned.

Other coastal castles in the Oban area, some in ruins and some preserved, are Dunollie, Dunstaffnage and Castle Stalker, while Duart Castle – opposite Oban on the Isle of Mull – controlled the seaways for Clan Maclean.

BELOW: *Caledonian camping coach overlooking Loch Awe, accessed by the station footbridge. The old green and cream livery of the West Highland has been retained.*

reaching Dalmally (population 550) as first stop. The station there opened in 1877, three years before the line to Oban was completed, but had to be rebuilt after a fire in 1898. In 2013 it was refurbished under ScotRail's 'Adopt a Station' scheme, while the main buildings, bought privately, contain Heartfelt by Liz (a feltwork craft studio) and offer private rooms to let: the old gentlemen's waiting room is now the Rambler's Rest, and the former animal pens next to the platform are now the Shepherd's Hut. (One room in the original 1877 station was for the private use of the Duke of Argyll, Chief of Clan Campbell, whose estate spreads across much of Argyll. The railway company proposed a branch line from Dalmally down to Inveraray, the Argyll county town, which hosts the Duke's Castle, but the proposal was rejected in Parliament.)

After Dalmally, as the line crosses the head of Loch Awe, Kilchurn Castle comes into view, providing an iconic view of a former Highland stronghold.

Classic loch view: West Highland Line Tyndrum– Oban skirts Loch Awe, here passing close to the shore behind St Conan's Kirk.

Loch Awe

Just two minutes after providing views of Kilchurn Castle, the train pulls into Loch Awe station, described by 'Friends of the West Highland Line' as a 'wayside halt', right beside the loch. The station buildings have gone, but a 'camping coach' provides backpacker accommodation where a second platform would be. The first such camping coach – a converted passenger car – was installed here back in 1952 under British Rail, although the camping coaches were a common sight at stations in holiday areas from the 1930s to the 1960s. Today, this type

KIRKS (CHURCHES) IN THE HIGHLANDS

Railway stations in town centres in the Highlands are likely to be situated close to at least one of the many churches or 'kirks' in the region. Most typical are the small kirks bearing the simple, almost puritanical elements of the 'Wee Free' branch of the Presbyterian church. However, larger towns and cities have cathedrals or large parish kirks of the Church of Scotland, together with those of other denominations (for example episcopal or Roman Catholic).

The Church of Scotland (Reformed Presbyterian) has been the country's established church since the Reformation of 1560, led by John Knox, but later tolerance allowed the revival of Catholic worship and the spread of other Christian denominations.

St Conan's on Loch Awe is one of those kirks built in the heyday of the Victorian era of expensive, elaborate public buildings drawing on past influences. The austerity of the early Presbyterian halls gave way in the nineteenth century to churches with multiple chapels, stained-glass windows and imported organs. Some notable cathedral-style churches accessible from Highlands railway stations are St Machar's, Aberdeen; St John's, Perth; the Episcopal Cathedral in Inverness; and St Columba's in Oban.

Railways were welcomed most fully 'into the body of the kirk' (or vice versa) at Roy Bridge and Rannoch on the West Highland Line, where station waiting rooms were used to host services on alternate Sundays.

of accommodation suits backpackers and hikers rather than families. Scotlandrailholiday.com is the website for the Caledonian Camping Coach Company, which owns the Loch Awe camping coach: 'The evening spent gazing at the loch and castle from the comfort of my pillow was totally memorable.' 'A wonderful concept. We enjoyed being the Railway Children. Great fun!'.

The original purpose of Loch Awe station was very different to the camping coach concept: it was built in 1881 to serve the adjacent luxury hotel, now owned by Lochs & Glens Holidays, a coach touring company with its own hotels whose coaches are a familiar sight on Highlands trunk roads throughout the year. Victorian pleasure seekers could stay at the Loch Awe Hotel, or join a steamship that would take them to other hotels around the loch, some of which are still trading today, such as Taycreggan and Ardanaiseig.

Loch Awe is also the stop for visiting St Conan's Kirk, described on the 'Undiscovered Scotland' website as 'magnificent, beautiful, remarkable, eccentric, and just a little bizarre' with its 'melange of spires, towers and turrets'. Built between 1881 and 1886 but elaborated after 1907, the Church of Scotland edifice was designed and paid for by a local Campbell family who attended the church themselves; the arrival of the nearby railway line meant that a larger congregation could be anticipated.

After Loch Awe station, the line hugs the waterside and affords further views down and across Scotland's longest freshwater loch (25 miles).

Falls of Cruachan

Five minutes along the River Awe valley is a seasonal stop at the Falls of Cruachan, which closed under Beeching in 1965 but reopened in 1988.

The anglicized name 'Falls' (that is, waterfalls) derived from Allt Cruachan, which originally flowed down in spectacular fashion from the towering Ben Cruachan (3,694ft). Their flow was interrupted in 1965 with the creation of a reservoir on the mountain to feed into Cruachan Power Station, Scotland's largest hydroelectric power station (capacity 440

HIGHLAND POWER AND THE RAILWAYS

Cruachan is one of over ninety major hydroelectric schemes across Scotland, and one of four 'pumped storage' schemes: water from the falls above the power station drives its turbines, and at times of low demand for electricity on the grid, water is pumped back up the pipes – a cheap process – for use at times of high demand.

Energy has always been integral to railways. The transport of coal was a primary justification for building early railways, which, under steam traction, were also an important customer for the coal mines. Longannet, in Fife, Scotland's last remaining coal-fired power station, closed in 2016; of interest to railway watchers, the Spanish train company, Talgo, soon after announced plans to open a large factory on the site.

Hydroelectricity was an obvious choice for the wet and windy Highlands, with dozens of schemes opening up after World War II. Since then, 'renewable' has come into use to describe 'green' energy, and Scotland has invested in hydro-power but also into wind and wave power, and biofuels.

The West Highland Line serves Cruachan and also, by Loch Lomond, passes close to the Loch Sloy pumped storage station.

megawatts). Mini-buses take visitors (50,000 a year) deep into the 'hollow mountain' to see the workings of Cruachan's pumped storage system.

Trains only stop at Falls of Cruachan in spring and summer, and then only in daylight hours because there is no electric lighting – a paradoxical feature of the station, given its location!

The Pass of Brander

Leaving Cruachan, the train enters the deep section of the River Awe valley known as the Pass of Brander. Famous for hosting a battle involving Robert the Bruce in 1308, the pass also has an interesting railway history. As secretary of Callander & Oban, John Anderson installed a warning system against the danger of rockfalls on the track in the pass. 'Anderson's piano' was a steel wire fence that hummed in the wind while sending signals along the track if a falling boulder broke a wire in the fence. Anderson has been widely credited by historians as the individual who saw through the difficult process of building the Callander & Oban: 'He was the man who created the railway almost single-handed, selling shares on the doorstep like a brush salesman, and inducing hoteliers to promote railway excursions' (*North of Scotland*, by John Thomas and David Turnock).

Moving out of the Pass of Brander, several other reminders of Highland industrial (and railway) history are encountered as the line runs parallel to Loch Etive. Bonawe Iron Furnace was an eighteenth-century iron-ore smelter that produced cannonballs for the Napoleonic Wars, while Inverawe Smokery has produced smoked salmon, a widely exported Scottish delicacy, since 1980.

Taynuilt

Taynuilt (population 800), on the south side of Loch Etive, was served by a car ferry across Airds Bay until 1966. In that year, Connel Bridge – a few miles down the road – was fully opened to road traffic, making the ferry superfluous. (The bridge had originally been built for the Connel–Ballachulish railway, which ended in 1966: *see* 'Lost Line Connel–Ballachulish', below.)

Connel Ferry and Beyond

The station at Connel still carries the name Connel Ferry despite the absence of ferries, although this remains a busy corner of the Highlands for transport and tourism. On the south side of the bridge are Connel Ferry railway station, the A85 (Oban to Perth trunk road), the A828 crossing the bridge (towards Fort William), and a large hotel, the Falls of Lora, opened in 1894. (The 'Falls' are actually unusual rapids in the shallows of Loch Etive, created by tides as the loch-end narrows to meet Loch Linnhe.) On the other side of the Connel Bridge is Oban's modest airport, offering several flights a week to equally

Connel Bridge, today a road bridge but originally (1903) built for the railway to Ballachulish; it crosses the foot of Loch Etive and the Falls of Lora tidal feature.

modest island destinations (Coll, Colonsay, Islay and Tiree).

Beyond Connel, if travelling by road (the A85), there is a noticeable increase of human activity as the outskirts of Oban are reached: side roads to Dunstaffnage and Dunollie castles, as well as hotels and restaurants and a handsome marina. This route along the coast would have been the logical railway route into Oban but for local disagreements. 'Money talked', so the line diverged inland and now passes through inland, suburban Oban before reaching its terminus.

The obvious necessity for this line to the coast was to reach a harbour for transferring goods and passengers to ships, but a railway line along the seafront would have spoiled the sea views for which so many tourists came to Oban, so a railway pier was built at the southern end of town. One famous objector to the North Pier not being chosen for a station was its owner, the businessman John Stuart McCaig. He became known for building McCaig's Tower (or Folly), an incomplete Colosseum-like granite structure on the hill above Oban.

Oban – Gateway to the Isles

We breathe the salt air as we take in the scene outside the station entrance: lively lads and lasses, a pipe band in the distance, the Macbrayne steamers waiting.

The Romance of Scotland's Railways by David St John Thomas and Patrick Whitehouse

Oban trains stop in a modernized railway station next to the modern ferry terminal, which offers regular crossings to eleven of the Hebrides, giving Oban its nickname of 'Gateway to the Isles'. The closest are Kerrera, Lismore and Mull (and onwards to Iona), with longer crossings (up to five hours) to Islay and Barra.

The town is also a hub for both local and long-distance buses and coaches run by Scottish Citylink and West Coast Motors, plus a variety of sea excursions from the harbour, in addition to the car-carrying ferries.

Oban's resident population is 8,500, but this can treble in the peak summer months, multiplied by tourists awaiting their ferry, taking in the sea breeze on Corran Esplanade, or sampling the town's many seafood restaurants. Visitor numbers also increase when Oban hosts the Royal National Mod, a traditional music festival, as it has done on many occasions.

All Aboard! Oban Station

A grand opening ceremony celebrated the opening of Oban station on 30 June 1880. The original building was replaced in 1986, despite its architectural listing, but the modernized station generally fits in with an updated, busy ferry terminal (itself upgraded in 2005). The station is surrounded by high street shopping, hotels, pubs and restaurants, the latter featuring many renowned fish-and-chips and seafood outlets, and all within walking distance.

Leaving the station on foot takes the passenger quickly, in various directions, to the ferry terminal; past a large, perpetually busy Wetherspoons pub (The Corryvreckan) and the highly rated Oban Seafood Hut; or immediately on Station Road to the heart of the town at Argyll Square.

The seafront end of Station Road is occupied by the massive Perle Oban Hotel, the original Station Hotel of Victorian times.

Lost Line: Connel–Ballachulish

Ballachulish is a small town (population 640) situated on Loch Leven, 30 miles from Connel up the coast of Loch Linnhe. The line from Connel was mainly built to service the big slate quarry near Ballachulish, but it also freighted bauxite, the rock mineral used to make aluminium, for part of its journey to the smelters at Fort William and Kinlochleven.

The single-track line – which closed in 1966 – also served passengers who lived in hamlets and villages such as Benderloch, Barcaldine and Creagan, where the old station is preserved as a house. Appin was the historic name of this district – ruled by the noble Stuarts of Appin – and there were stops at Duror and Kentallen (whose station is now part of the Holly Tree Hotel) before arriving at Ballachulish. South and North Ballachulish are separated by the mouth of Loch Leven.

The terminus was named 'Ballachulish (Glencoe)' for most of its life, suggesting that it is the nearest railway station to Glencoe, the valley famous for its beauty and historic resonance. The buildings themselves were converted into a health centre. Part of the old line is used as a Sustrans cycle route.

Services on the Crianlarich–Oban Line

The ScotRail timetables for May to December 2019 (to 14 December) featured six journeys from Crianlarich (trains all starting in Glasgow) on the West Highland Line, and four on Sundays. The earliest Glasgow departures for Oban were 5.20 Mon.–Sat. (arr. Oban 8.35) and 8.54 on Sundays.

The pocket-sized West Highlands timetable also usefully includes ferry connections to the islands run by 'CalMac' from Oban to Castlebay, Mull, Lismore, Colonsay, Coll and Tiree. For example, a through journey on a Tuesday (daily times differ during the week) from Glasgow to Tiree could be seen at a glance, starting by West Highland Line in Glasgow Queen Street at 10.33, reaching Oban station at 13.43, picking up the 15.00 ferry to Coll (17.40) and arriving at Tiree at 18.50.

Journeys to the Coast (2): Fort William to Mallaig

> On the opening day, 1 April 1901, steamers and trains converged on the tiny village of Mallaig....the people that morning were witnessing the birth of a new port [and] of a private railway company.
>
> (*North of Scotland* by John Thomas and David Turnock)

The Fort William–Mallaig route has become more famous than its financiers and constructors could ever have conceived thanks to the Harry Potter books! Visits to Glenfinnan station, halfway down the line, have more than doubled because film of *The Jacobite* steam train crossing the Glenfinnan

Viaduct was featured in the Harry Potter movies. However, the line is shared by ScotRail's regular service with West Coast Railways, the private company that operates *The Jacobite*.

The origins of the West Highland in Glasgow were detailed in Chapter 6, and the branch from Tyndrum to Oban was described earlier in this chapter. Passengers who stay on the train all the way to Fort William, the original line terminus, have the option of continuing their journey to Glenfinnan, or to go all the way to Mallaig using either ScotRail or *The Jacobite*.

Heading northwards from Fort William (the town was profiled in Chapter 6), the line starts out on the West Highland track, but divides half-a-mile out to cross the River Lochy (flowing into Loch Linnhe) and the Caledonian Canal, and then heads directly westwards.

The Caledonian Canal and Local Stations

The Caledonian Canal, the brainchild of engineer Thomas Telford, runs for 60 miles north-west from Fort William to Inverness, linking five lochs including Loch Linnhe (at Fort William) and Loch Ness (at Inverness). The canal was constructed between 1803 and 1822 (by navigators, or 'navvies'), but within a few years of its opening it was threatened by rail as the more efficient method of long-distance transport, for goods or humans. Today the canal is used primarily for leisure.

Where the canal descends to Loch Linnhe, a series of locks – called Neptune's Staircase – was needed to accommodate differing heights above sea level, and this is also a feature at the town of Fort Augustus, on the way to Inverness.

Banavie

Neptune's Staircase is at a village called Banavie, which was given a station as an extension to the West Highland Line to Fort William (opened in 1895). The station served goods and passengers transferring to steamers on the canal, and was renamed Banavie Pier when the more direct station to Banavie, on the Mallaig line, opened in 1901.

At Banavie there is a swing bridge to allow watercraft to access the Caledonian Canal or Loch Linnhe.

Just after Banavie, trains cross a swing bridge over the canal, which was needed to allow masted vessels through; from the bridge, there are views up the eight locks that make up Neptune's Staircase.

Corpach

The line then curves directly westwards to stop at Corpach, and runs past a few industrial sites – one is a large sawmill owned by BSW Timber, 'the largest integrated forestry business in the UK'. Corpach was used in World War II as a repair base for Royal Navy ships.

On this line, the stations closest to Fort William are used mainly by locals, including children heading for several schools in the area: Lochaber High is the region's only high school with a roll of 800 students drawn from a dozen small primary schools.

After Corpach, views to the left open out over the first of several lochs on this scenic journey on a run of fifteen minutes. Homes near the lochside are served by Loch Eil Outward Bound (in both directions) and, on request, Locheilside.

Glenfinnan Viaduct

Half-an-hour out of Fort William comes the climax of this journey for both Harry Potter fans and railway enthusiasts: the crossing of Glenfinnan Viaduct before arriving at Glenfinnan station. Supported by twenty-one arches, 100 feet high, the concrete viaduct runs in a twelve-chain curve for 416 yards over the steep valley of the River Finnan just before it empties into Loch Shiel. According to the story in *History of Concrete: A Very Old and Modern Material* by Jahren Per and Sui Tongbo, hundreds of carpenters were needed to make the timber scaffolding and formwork for building the viaduct; legend has it that a horse and cart slipped off the scaffolding and fell deep into one of the piers, and they were buried in the pillar as it was impossible to extract them. (In fact modern investigations have revealed the remains of a horse and cart within a pier of Loch Nan Uamh Viaduct, further down the line to Mallaig, but not at Glenfinnan.)

Opened with the line in 1901, Glenfinnan Viaduct was designed by Robert McAlpine, who took part in the initial planning for the main West Highland Line (*see* 'The Rannoch Moor survey 1889' in Chapter 6). McAlpine had earned the nickname 'Concrete Bob' for pioneering the use of concrete instead of quarried stone, as in most previous Highland structures.

Views down from the viaduct – either from the train itself, or if walking on foot to its base from the Glenfinnan Visitor Centre – are as picturesque as those looking upwards to the viaduct from below; you can see down Glen Shiel for several miles on a clear day, with the Glenfinnan monument in the foreground. A new footpath for viewing the viaduct was opened in 2019 (together with a café hut).

The Glenfinnan area was already famous in Highland Scotland history, but at the end of the twentieth century it was catapulted to international fame as the location for the filming of author J.K. Rowling's 'Harry Potter' books (released between 1997 and 2007). These books comprise one of the world's best-selling series, while the eight movies made up one of the most lucrative film franchises of all time. Shots of Glenfinnan Viaduct being crossed by the fictional Hogwarts Express steam train – in reality, *The Jacobite* – on the way to Hogwarts wizard school appeared in the first four Warner Brothers movies.

The Glen first became famous as the meeting point for rebel clans under Bonnie Prince Charlie, in July 1745. The Bonnie Prince was Charles Edward Stuart (1720–88), the Young Pretender to the British throne on behalf of his father, James Stuart – the Old Pretender – both exiled in France. The Prince landed in the Highlands, gathered a rebel army of 'Jacobites' and marched south, seizing Edinburgh and reaching the English Midlands before retreating and suffering defeat at the Battle of Culloden, near Inverness.

Glenfinnan: seventeen of the twenty-one concrete arches that make up the magnificent viaduct, propelled to global fame by the Harry Potter movies. ISTOCK. COM/DAVID BOUTIN PHOTOGRAPHY

The 60-foot high Glenfinnan monument to this event looks out over Loch Shiel, accessed from the National Trust for Scotland (NTS) visitor centre on the A830 road that runs alongside the railway line. Visitors can climb the monument and see an exhibition about Bonnie Prince Charlie's rebellion.

Glenfinnan Station, and Beyond

The stop at Glenfinnan station itself comes two-thirds of a mile after crossing the viaduct. The station's down platform has a small museum, run by volunteers, installed in 1991 and upgraded in 2013, telling the story of the West Highland Line.

Beyond Glenfinnan, both ScotRail and *Jacobite* passengers enjoy a scenic run climbing the hills inland alongside the A830 until the ways divide, the road taking the north bank of Loch Eilt, and the railway diverging to run along the south bank for 3 miles.

At the end of Loch Eilt, rail and road meet again to run alongside River Ailort, flowing west into Loch Ailort. There is a request stop (Lochailort) within the former Inverailort estate, which once had its own private stop (Lech-a-vuie Platform) for shooting parties heading for nearby Inverailort House.

Next, the railway skirts little Loch Dubh ('dark lake') on a stretch where the difficulties of surmounting terrain problems become apparent, the train passing through deep cuttings or tunnels carved into the tough ancient rock, or across bridges and viaducts. The two large viaducts needed here – both by McAlpine, in concrete – cross over the Arnabol Burn (six 50-foot wide spans) and, at the head of Loch nan Uamh, over Allt a'Mhama (Mama Burn), using eight 50-foot arches with a concrete pylon in the middle.

Loch Ailort and nan Uamh are sea lochs, inlets leading out to the Sound of Arisaig and then into the North Atlantic. A roadside sign marks the way to the Prince's Cairn, a stack of rocks that commemorates the actual landing here of Bonnie Prince Charlie.

Beasdale is a request stop that was built principally to serve Arisaig House, a base for paramilitary training in World War II, now operating as a country house hotel. An earlier house, Borrodale, provided lodgings for the Bonnie Prince but was later destroyed by government troops in a reprisal after Culloden. At Borrodale, a viaduct of that name features a single span of no less than 127 feet, which set a world record for a concrete bridge in 1896.

A scenic stretch along the south shoreline of Loch Eilt. SRPS

'The Jacobite steam train approaching Morar Station', and Morar Hotel (the largest white building). Views west across Silver Sands towards the mountains on Skye. NORMAN MCNAB

Arisaig

Alighting at Arisaig station entails a five-minute walk down to the centre of the village. Although small, with a population of just 300, the village is locally important for its connections by road and rail, and its community facilities: the Spar general store and post office; the Land, Sea & Islands Centre, with tourist information, a shop and events; and Astley Hall, for céilidhs (country dances), parties, concerts, weddings and produce fairs.

Arisaig is the most westerly of all stations in Britain – even beating Penzance, in Cornwall – and the railway line veers northwards here, away from sea views to the west, but providing views to the east up Loch Morar, which is dotted with many small islands (*eileans*). Loch Morar is publicised in guide books as home to 'Morag', a rival monster to Nessie, but the loch is more reliably proclaimed as Britain's deepest lake, going down to 1,107 feet. Another claim to fame is that the River Morar, which empties from the loch to the sea, is Scotland's shortest river, at less than a mile long.

Morar

As the train bridges the river over a four-arched viaduct, there are views east of the River Morar's estuary, with beaches known as the 'Silver (sometimes 'White') Sands of Morar'. There are camping and caravanning sites here, and the beaches have appeared in films such as *Local Hero* (1983, Bill Forsyth), *Breaking the Waves* (1996, Lars von Trier) and television's *Monarch of the Glen* (2005). The station buildings at Morar itself are used by a local publisher to produce *West Word*, a local community newspaper.

On the final run from Morar to Mallaig, the Isle of Skye comes into view to the north, while views westwards open out impressively towards islands known as the 'Small Isles' – Rum, Eigg (pronounced 'egg'), Muck and little Canna (tucked away beyond Rum). All four islands, once home to crofting families who emigrated, are now looked after as nature reserves.

Mallaig

The Isle of Skye, in contrast to the Small Isles, is the largest island of the Inner Hebrides and Scotland's most populous island, with 10,000 residents (although before the nineteenth century, twice as many lived on the island). Its southern peninsula, Sleat (pronounced 'slate'), is connected to the mainland – across the Sound of Sleat – by a regular, busy ferry service from Mallaig, the terminus of this line from Fort William.

Mallaig (with a population of 1,000) has the buzzing activity of a port, with two harbours, and fishing and other working vessels coming to and fro, along with the CalMac ferries and private excursion boats to Skye and the Small Isles, together with plentiful accommodation and catering.

All Aboard! Mallaig Station

At the station, there is a chance to photograph the gently steaming *Jacobite* arriving or waiting to depart; arrivals are greeted by the welcome smell of fish and chips from Jaffy's Shop within the station buildings. 'Jaffy' Lawrie also set up an important fish-curing business in the town, which continues today.

Mallaig station was adopted by Sonia Cameron, a former British Rail catering worker, who went on to beautify two other local stations (Arisaig and Morar) with hanging baskets and whisky-cask planters.

Next to the station exit is the local museum, Mallaig Heritage Centre, where it is revealed that the town barely existed until the railway arrived. The laird, Lord Lovat and Chief of Clan Fraser, set up a fishing village for peasant farmers who were

Early days (photo, 1914) at Mallaig (the line was completed in 1901), when the track continued on to the pier (until 1968). SRPS

being 'cleared' from his lands in the middle of the nineteenth century, but growth was galvanized in the 1890s by the prospect of a railway link:

> The new harbour was far closer to the rich fishing grounds west of Barra than either of the other railheads at Oban and Kyle of Lochalsh, and fishing vessels were quick to exploit the possibility of getting their catches to market faster. A concrete breakwater was built as part of the railway infrastructure, and fish were loaded directly into wagons on the quay ready to be taken south.
>
> Mallaig Heritage Centre website

Services on the Fort William–Mallaig Line

In 2019 (from May to December), ScotRail ran four daily departures from Fort William to Mallaig (Mon.–Sat.) and three on Sunday. A 'through' journey from Glasgow, starting from Queen Street at 12.24, would involve a twelve-minute wait at Crianlarich (for the Oban half of the train to uncouple and depart), a 14.24 departure from Crianlarich, arriving 16.09 at Fort William, then changing to the Mallaig service departing ten minutes later (16.19) to arrive at Mallaig at 17.43.

The ScotRail timetable covering West Highland services has two useful features in connection with this line:

- The times for the West Coast Railway ('Jacobite Steam Train') from Fort William and Mallaig (twice daily in both directions, seven days a week in summer). For an excursion example, passengers could board the 10.15 from Fort William to arrive at 12.25 in Mallaig, returning on the 14.10 – or for a longer stay in Mallaig, on the 18.38 (arriving at Fort William at 20.31). Many choose the option of a one-way trip by steam, returning on the faster ScotRail service
- Ferry connections (CalMac) from Mallaig, principally to Armadale on the Isle of Skye (a forty-five-minute sail) but also, less frequently, to the Small Isles (Eigg, Muck, Rum and Canna)

Journey to the Coast (3): Dingwall to Kyle of Lochalsh on the 'Kyle Line'

> The views from the window are worth the fare alone.
>
> Friends of the Kyle Line website

A postcard printed for Highland Railway showing HR 85, a Class L or 'Skye Bogie', built in 1892, waiting to head eastwards from the Kyle of Lochalsh terminus. SRPS

Like the Callander & Oban line, Dingwall & Skye took many years to complete a full line, with construction encountering both physical and human resistance along the way. Despite the mention of 'Skye' in the original company, the line from Dingwall terminated at Stromeferry in 1870, and another twenty-seven years passed before it reached Kyle of Lochalsh, close to the Isle of Skye. (An impressive single-span crossing, the Skye bridge originally charged a toll – it was built under a private finance initiative – but local protests ended the toll in 2004.)

As the Inverness to Kyle Line, the service survived the Beeching cuts, despite low traffic then and today, the 'Kyle line' offering four daily through-services (Mon.–Fri.) from Inverness to Kyle of Lochalsh. Inverness to Dingwall was open by 1862; that station – also a junction for the Far North Line – was detailed earlier, in Chapter 5. The printed ScotRail timetable brings the two lines together under 'North Highlands'.

As on the Far North, there are a fair number of 'request' stops on the Kyle Line. This is because both lines are characterized by sheer distances between isolated stations and a scattered human population. Kyle of Lochalsh is 80 miles from Inverness, and six of the eleven stations are request stops, indicating the sparsity of inhabitation on this east–west crossing through the north-west Highlands.

Garve

Leaving Dingwall westbound, this sparsity is quickly illustrated by the long, twenty-three minute run to the first stop, Garve, through open countryside and a run alongside Loch Garve. (By Garve, the train is already nearly an hour out of Inverness.) However, an explanation for the long, quiet run is the absence of a stop at Strathpeffer, a relatively large community for this region, which lost its station in 1946 (see 'Lost Line: Strathpeffer, a Victorian Spa Town' below).

In railway nostalgia, Garve could have been the start of a branch line off the Dingwall & Skye that never got beyond the proposal stage; it would have run north-westwards to the port of Ullapool through 32 miles of lochside and wilderness. Instead it is the A835 road that branches off near Garve, while the railway line continues parallel to the A832, directly west towards Achnasheen. (Backpackers taking the train as far as Garve can use an infrequent bus service on the A835, Inverness to Ullapool, to then catch the ferry to the island of Lewis.)

After Garve come two request stops, Lochluichart and Achanalt, and then a scenic, if lonely, run along the valley of Strath Bran, tracking alongside the River Bran and the A832, the only A road through this territory. The Bran name for valley and river recalls the Brahan Seer, sometimes nicknamed the Scottish Nostradamus, who laboured on the Seaforth estate in the seventeenth century but had 'the sight' to predict cataclysmic events, including the arrival of the railway (or something like it) through his homeland.

The day will come when long strings of carriages without horses shall run between Dingwall and Inverness, and more wonderful still, between Dingwall and the Isle of Skye.

The Prophecies of the Brahan Seer
by Alexander McKenzie

Achnasheen, and Beyond

Achnasheen ('village of storms' from the Gaelic) might be insignificant by population but, like Garve, its name is familiar to Highland travellers for its railway station and as a crossroads. The A890 branches south-westerly with the railway line, both destined for Kyle of Lochalsh, while the A832 continues westwards to Loch Maree and the coast at Gairloch and Poolewe. Like the Garve–Ullapool proposal, the dream of a railway from Achnasheen to Aultbea on the north-west coast was unrealistic and never materialized. Instead, there is a once-daily bus service from Achnasheen to Gairloch.

Achnashellach

Achnasheen's station hotel burnt down in 1996 so most passengers stay on the train through Glen Carron, and usually through the request station at Achnashellach ('field of the willows'), too, although some hill-walkers may disembark for walks

RAIL, BUS AND FERRY IN THE HIGHLANDS

It can be hard enough to keep abreast of rail timetable changes, let alone other public transport services, but there have been sporadic attempts at mapping the possible connections for intrepid travellers such as climbers, backpackers and island-hopping tourists. Application software and mobile phones have, of course, revolutionized the way young adults travel to and through remote areas.

Traveline Scotland is the official public–private partnership for connecting operators, with an efficient journey planner on its website, and a mobile app. For example, a search for Achnasheen to Portree on the island of Skye comes up with the Kyle Line train times, the walking route from Kyle station to the relevant bus stop, the bus number (916, 'reservation recommended', Glasgow–Uig route), and arrival time and place in Portree.

From Kyle to the island of Lewis, the suggested route is by rail to Garve, changing there (after fifty-two minutes) to bus 961 for the ferry terminal at Ullapool (a fifty-nine minute wait), and then taking the CalMac ferry to Stornoway on Lewis.

Other popular connections involving Highland railways and the islands are the various CalMac ferries from Oban to the Inner Hebrides; the Mallaig ferry to the Isle of Skye; from Scrabster, near Thurso, to Orkney; and the ferry from Aberdeen to Orkney and Shetland.

through Forestry Commission lands or north to the mountains of Torridon.

Strathcarron

Leaving Achnashellach alongside Loch Dughaill, over the River Carron, there is a sense of approaching the coast and of leaving the wilderness behind as the train pulls into Strathcarron station. This is the site of another important road junction, the A896 pulling away to the west alongside Loch Carron and, eventually, isolated Applecross and Shieldaig. Lochcarron Weavers – 'the world's leading manufacturer of tartan' – started here, although its factory is now in the Scottish Borders.

BELOW: *View to the future? Achnasheen station, now used by 3,500 passengers a year, from 2,500 in the early 2000s. This view is west from the footbridge across the River Bra. Note the shorter platform 2 (up, eastbound; next to the sheep field) and the longer platform 1 with the portable step (low platform).*

Attadale

The railway line continues alongside the A890 on the eastern side of Loch Carron, with a request stop at Attadale. The main reason for disembarking here would be to walk up to gardens that are open in the summer as part of the enormous Attadale estate (30,000 acres), for which the station was originally a private halt. The house at Attadale was featured in *Hamish Macbeth*, a popular 1990s television drama, with Robert Carlyle in the lead role as a village policeman.

Attadale's modern-day owners (on www.Attadale.com) are frank about the economics of a Highland estate: 'Most of the estate is bare hillside … such properties have to produce whatever income they can from a variety of sources' – this would include converting workers' cottages into holiday lets; leasing the farmland; offering fishing passes on the River Carron; and opening the gardens to the public.

Stromeferry

Stromeferry was the original terminus (opened in 1870) from Inverness and Dingwall because, as the name indicates, there used to be a steamer ferry across to Skye and even to Lewis. Sidings, signal boxes, an engine shed and a goods shed and yard with access to the pier made it a busy terminus in its day – in fact Stromeferry was too busy for some: on one Sunday in 1883 local Sabbatarians rioted against work being done on the Lord's Day, and in 1891 the shed was burned down, setting fire to a fourteen-carriage train waiting to depart.

The only indication left of Stromeferry's heyday is the large, former Stationmaster's Lodge, still operating under that name, which has group accommodation to hire ('sleeps up to twenty in comfort' – 2019 rates are from £350 per night for the whole house).

While Stromeferry was important, the intention of the railway investors was to reach Kyle of Lochalsh, but lack of finance for major engineering works held back the extension until 1897. Building the extension was a massive effort involving excavations for thirty separate cuttings and the building of twenty-nine bridges through steep slopes. The cost came to £20,000 per mile of track, making the Stromeferry–Kyle extension the costliest stretch of track in Britain up to that time.

Duncraig

After the compulsory stop at Stromeferry, the next is a request stop called Duncraig, named after the nearby castle and, like Attadale, originally the landowner's private halt. Even today, to reach the main road from the station, or vice versa, passengers must walk or drive through the castle gardens and pass immediately in front of the building itself. Due to reopen as a luxury 'B&B' in 2020 (rooms at £225 per night), Duncraig Castle was built by Sir Alexander Matheson, who, among other business interests, was chairman of the Dingwall & Skye Railway (later absorbed by Highland). (Jardine Matheson's 'other business interests' included profiting from opium trading in China; a plaster ceiling in the castle is carved with poppy flowers.)

As a public-use station, Duncraig was closed between 1964 and 1976, although during this period trains continued to pause there because drivers would not acknowledge its closure. Early this century, the castle itself attracted media attention when it was occupied by an English family filmed for *The Dobsons of Duncraig*, a BBC documentary, which captured feuding that tore the seventeen-strong family asunder.

To reach Duncraig, the railway line from Stromeferry has followed close to the shore of Loch Kishorn – a sea loch that is effectively the firth, or estuary, of Loch Carron – without a road running next to it for several miles (an unusual pattern, even in the remote Highlands).

Plockton

The next station serves Plockton, one of the most famous villages in the Highlands thanks to its media coverage. Proudly calling itself 'The Jewel of the Highlands', Plockton – a 'ploc' is a peninsula or promontory in Gaelic – has 400 inhabitants and plenty of tourist accommodation for its size. (Like Attadale, Plockton featured in the *Hamish Macbeth* television series.)

Duncraig's single platform looking west out over Loch Kishor; the line hugs the shore, separate from any roads, before heading inland to Plockton.

Situated near the High School and away from the village centre is Plockton's pretty station, built in 1887 under pitch-pine cladding. The main building was converted into a restaurant and later into a self-catering let called 'Off the Rails'. The lounge used to be the ticket office, and the sales hatch is preserved; one bedroom used to be the ladies' waiting room, while the gentlemen's equivalent has been converted into a kitchen/dining room.

After Plockton, Duirinish is a humble request stop serving the hamlet of the same name and other tiny settlements such as Drumbuie, Erbusaig and Badicaul. As at Plockton, the station is a few minutes' hike from the centre of the picturesque hamlet, where Highland cattle and sheep are free to roam.

Kyle of Lochalsh

The Kyle line terminates in its eponymous town of Kyle of Lochalsh. Once a busy ferry port, Kyle lost this role when the road bridge to Skye opened in 1995, but it remains significant as a port for marine activities and as a regional market town.

Kyle of Lochalsh station sits on the railway pier jutting out into the strait, a position that recalls the former role of the railways in connecting with ferries – and vessels can still dock close to the station. Room was created for several sidings, since freight would be important to and from the town – especially timber loads – and for a modest engine shed and a signal box (now a holiday let).

Modernization over the years has incorporated a restaurant – the highly rated Waterside Seafood

Restaurant – and a shop in the station buildings, together with a museum run by the 'Friends of the Kyle Line'.

Lost Line: Strathpeffer, a Victorian Spa Town

The Strathpeffer story is, in many ways, a microcosm of the history of Highland railways: difficult routes, intransigent landlords, but scenic journeys culminating at splendid hotels. The logical route westwards for the Dingwall & Skye would have run through, and served, Strathpeffer, at that time a thriving spa town (population today 1,500). But objections by a local landowner put the 1870 station at an impractical location outside the town until 1885, when a branch line into the town was agreed and a central station built.

Spas were popular across Europe, famous British examples including Bath and Harrogate (and Scotland's Bridge of Allan on the Highland Main Line). Taking the sulphurous spring waters at 'pump rooms' could occupy the wealthy leisure classes for several weeks, so large, luxurious hotels and boarding houses were built in these towns.

Victorian visitors would come from as far afield as London to 'take the waters' and stay in Strathpeffer's grand hotels, but the fashion faded in the twentieth century and the branch line closed in 1946. The big hotels are still there, including the Bay Highland, originally built for Highland Railway in 1911. So is the 1885 station, now occupied by the Highland

Visitor at Strathpeffer old station contemplates entering the Highland Museum of Childhood.

Museum of Childhood and a popular café. Work is being done to clear the old track as a walking route, called the Peffery Way.

Services on The Kyle Line

This journey is incorporated in the North Highlands timetable printed by ScotRail covering the Far North (to Wick and Thurso), as well as the west-bound line to Kyle. In 2019 (May–December), four services left Dingwall daily (Mon.–Sat.) for Kyle (the first at 9.29, the last at 18.29) and two on Sunday.

Transport connections are provided in the timetable leaflet:

- Stations served by local bus services ('at or near the stations'), such as Kyle of Lochalsh for Skye; Garve for Ullapool; and Dingwall for Strathpeffer and Contin
- Ferry services: although not on the Kyle Line, timings are shown using rail, bus and/or ferry from Edinburgh or Glasgow all the way through Inverness to Ullapool and the Western Isles

Sources for the Lines to The West Coast

(*See also* 'Sources' for general sources.)

Note: Sources are included that cover the whole of the West Highland system with its branches to Oban and Mallaig.

The History of the Railways of the Scottish Highlands (series 1977–1990):
    Originally published by David & Charles, now from House of Lochar, Isle of Colonsay
    1. Thomas, J., *The West Highland Railway*
    4. Thomas, J., *The Callander & Oban Railway*
    5. Thomas, J., *The Skye Railway [Inverness–Kyle line]*

Northern Books from Famedram Publishers:
    The Kyle Line in Pictures 2005
    The Mallaig Railway 2009
    The Story of the West Highland: The 1940s LNER Guide 2001 (reprint)

Kennedy, D., *The Birth and Death of a Highland Railway: The Ballachulish Line* (John Murray 1971)

McGregor, J., *The West Highland Line: Great Railway Journeys Through Time* (Amberley 2013)

Pearson, M., *Iron Road to the Isles: A Travellers' and Tourist Guide to the West Highland Line* (J.M. Pearson & Sons 2001)

Price, D., *The Kyle of Lochalsh and Far North Lines* (Amberley 2018)

Thomas, J. and Turnock, D., *A Regional History of the Railways of Great Britain, Vol 15: The North of Scotland* (David & Charles 1989)

Internet (www.)
Friends of the Kyle Line
(kylerailway.co.uk)

Friends of the West Highland Line
(westhighlandline.org.uk)

Railscot.co.uk – primary resource for Scottish railway information

ScotRail
(ScotRail.co.uk) – official website of Abellio franchise

scot-rail
(scot-rail.co.uk) – 'Scotland's online rail enthusiast community'

CHAPTER 8

Scottish Highland Railways in the Twentieth Century

The previous seven chapters have covered a period of approximately seventy years in Scottish railway history (from 1830 to 1900), but only one chapter will cover the ensuing period of roughly ninety years (1903 to 1990). The reasons for this disparity are threefold:

- By 1903, the network of railway lines across the Highlands had been completed; the twentieth century would only see contraction of this pattern, concentrated in the 1960s
- Events and trends affecting Highland railways in the twentieth century would, in large part, be the same as those affecting the whole of what became 'British Rail': less detail, line by line, is needed
- Third, the broad sweep of twentieth-century events shaping British railways has been adequately covered in numerous other publications, old and new: repetition here would be unwarranted

A chronology of the companies that started the nineteenth-century railways, many of which survived into the twentieth century, is presented in Appendix III. To set the scene from 1903 onwards, a selection of dates will suffice:

- 1831 (Dundee & Newtyle) through to 1860: 'railway mania' sees companies start up in most parts of the Highlands, especially serving Aberdeen, Inverness, Perth and Dundee. Inverness and Aberdeen were connected
- 1860s: 'absorptions' (mergers and acquisitions, in today's corporate language) bring together many independent lines under common ownership (or running powers), leading to the emergence of the much larger Highland Railway, Great North, Caledonian and North British groups
- 1870s and 1880s: completion of many projects, connecting Caithness, Stromeferry, Oban and other termini
- 1890s–1903: 'direct' Highland Main completed; the West Highland, as far as Mallaig; Kyle reached; over-ambitious lines: Invergarry & Fort Augustus, the Ballachulish branch

The New Century: Plunged into World War

The year 1903 brought the last opening of new lines in the Highlands, almost coincidentally within two weeks of each other: Spean Bridge via Invergarry to Fort Augustus, and Connel Bridge to Ballachulish. The former line had originally been part of a grandiose plan, thwarted by corporate competition, to

THE JELLICOE EXPRESS

During World War I (1914–18), trains named 'Jellicoe Express' transported soldiers from London all the way to Thurso where they joined the Grand Fleet based on Scapa Flow, or alighted at Invergordon for the naval base there. The name 'Jellicoe Express' was after Sir John, 1st Earl Jellicoe (1859–1935), Admiral of the Fleet during World War I.

Scapa Flow, a natural sea harbour south of mainland Orkney, was used as the Royal Navy's main base in both World Wars.

Plaques commemorating the Jellicoe Express have been put up at various stations along the route. In the Flow Country (around Forsinard), sphagnum moss was harvested to be used as antiseptic dressings by the military.

Soldiers passing through some stations (including Dingwall and Perth) on the 'Jellicoe' were provided with refreshment by local volunteers.

Plaque seen at Far North stations commemorating the 'Jellicoe Express', the nickname for the trains that took soldiers and seamen to Thurso (and Scapa Flow).

connect Fort William all the way through the Great Glen to Inverness. That foundered ambition was the great 'what might have been' of Scottish Highland railways.

With all lines completed, it might be fair to consider the early 1900s – the Edwardian era under a new king, Edward VII (1841–1910) – as the 'golden age' of rail in Scotland. Certainly train travel was becoming more luxurious, with the likes of Pullman cars and refreshment rooms at stations delineated by class. Luxury hotels contributed to the improving image across Scotland: there were railway-owned hotels at Perth, Aberdeen and Inverness, while Edinburgh suddenly boasted two five-star hotels: the North British (1902; now the Balmoral) and the Caledonian (1903; now Waldorf Astoria).

But problems lurked around the corner in the early 1900s. Workers were becoming more demanding, if not yet militant; the motor car had appeared as a threat; and 1914 suddenly brought the national emergency of a European, later global, war. As noted by David Ross in *Getting the Train*, the British government imposed a Railway Executive Committee to oversee wartime transport, and Highland lines were heavily involved, for instance in transporting mines (Dingwall to Kyle, Alness to Invergordon) and moving troops on the 'Jellicoe Express' from Euston to Thurso (for Scapa Flow).

'Grouping'

The war years persuaded the government that a more consolidated railway industry would be beneficial: the first Ministry of Transport was set up in 1919, although nationalization was not seriously considered. There was a suggestion that Scotland could have a single company separate from England, which would have had enormous repercussions. Instead, Britain's railways were forced to consolidate the 'Grouping' into a Big Four.

Appendix II lays out the history of Scotland's independent railways, which became part of the Big Four. In terms of the Highlands, LMS (London Midland & Scottish) absorbed Caledonian and Highland, while LNER (London & North Eastern Railway) absorbed North British and Great North of Scotland. Both enlarged companies competed in the central and eastern Highland areas, but LMS was dominant (through Highland) in the far north, while LNER controlled the west (West Highland) while maintaining a strong grip in Grampian. In the Big Four, Great Western and Southern only operated in England and Wales.

Following four years of lively discussion after World War I, the Grouping came into being on 1 January 1923 (under the Railways Act, 1921). More years would be needed to rebrand as LMS or LNER all the equipment used by Scotland's independents, from stations, signage and uniforms to rolling stock. It was also necessary to reassure the travelling public, so corporate image became important, from staff training through to colour schemes for liveries.

Depression, War and Nationalization (British Railways)

The Great Depression naturally coloured the 1930s as a decade, and railways everywhere had to adapt to economic stringencies. Meanwhile, competition was increasing from the roads for both passenger transport – buses and coaches – and freight – lorries and trucks.

Necessity was the mother of invention, however, at the Big Four rail companies, and they employed engineers who would become celebrities in railway history. Sir Nigel Gresley (1876–1941) was one of these: he was born in Edinburgh – a plaque commemorates him at Edinburgh Waverley station – but only because his mother was visiting a gynaecologist in the Scottish capital; he grew up and worked in England. Gresley had already had a distinguished career as Chief Mechanical Engineer at LNER since Grouping, and he continued to design fast and striking locomotives into the 1930s, not least the *Flying Scotsman* within his A1 Pacific range, and *Mallard*, the fastest steam locomotive ever built.

The 'Flying Scotsman' brand was (and still is) a

service (London to Edinburgh), rather than a loco-motive, although LNER Class A3 4472, one of the Pacifics designed by Sir Nigel in 1923, coined the name. The service terminates in Edinburgh, not the Highlands, but the branding undoubtedly encour-aged many English travellers to head for Scotland by train.

William Stanier was another design engineer of that era whose name became associated with inno-vative locomotives at LMS, such as the Black 5 series.

While the exciting new generation of steam engines was attracting attention, the 1930s also saw the introduction of early diesel traction and further advances in electric traction. But it was streamlined, steam locomotives that captured the imagination, not least the 'Coronation Scot' class, which, like other long-distance trains, featured on the London–Glasgow or London–Edinburgh routes, but nevertheless helped simultaneously to glamor-ize rail travel, and Scotland as a destination.

Mallard set its 126mph record in July 1938, but Europe was already hurtling towards another World War, taking the railway system and the Scottish Highlands with it. As had happened in World War I, the railways came under government control in World War II, and this was one factor in the political decision, after the war, to nationalize the industry. For the Scottish Highlands (and Scot-land generally), this brought to an end the era in which two of the private Big Four operators control-led the railways. Instead, a Scottish Region was created within the new British Railways (later British Rail).

In retrospect, control of railways in the Scottish Highlands had progressively been moved further away from the Highlands themselves, where proud 'local' companies had been formed a hundred years earlier in Aberdeen and Inverness. From 1948, ulti-mate control lay with the government in London, although rail was far from being uniquely 'national-ized'. Health care, airlines, iron and steel, telecom-munications, coal mining and electricity generation all went through a similar process between 1945 and 1951. This included the nationalization, in 1943, of the North of Scotland Hydro-Electricity Board, closest to the Highlands.

THE PRINCIPAL BEECHING CLOSURES IN THE HIGHLANDS, 1964–68

LINE	YEAR[1]	RAILWAY COMPANY[2]
Aberdeen–Ballater	1966	Deeside[3]
Arbroath–Forfar	1967	Arbroath & Forfar
Brechin–Kinnaber Junction	1967	Aberdeen (Caledonian)
Callander–Oban	1965	Callander & Oban/West Highland
Craigellachie–Boat of Garten	1965	Strathspey[3]
Crieff–Comrie	1964	Crieff & Comrie
Dunblane–Callander	1965	Dunblane, Doune & Callander
Dyce–Peterhead	1965	Great North of Scotland
Elgin–Lossiemouth/Craigellachie	1966	Morayshire
Forres–Aviemore	1965	Inverness & Perth Junction
Keith–Elgin (via Dufftown)	1968	Keith & Dufftown[3]
Kintore–Alford	1966	Alford Valley branch
Macduff–Inveramsay	1966	Banff, Portsoy & Strathisla
Perth–Crieff	1967	Crieff & Methven Junction

[1] Closure of line to passengers in 1960s (some lost freight in earlier years or retained freight after the year shown)

[2] Original company; part of British Rail by the 1960s

[3] Part of line or stations preserved as heritage lines

Note: the loss of these lines, and their original creation, is described as part of the previous chapters on specific Highland lines

Modernization and Rationalization (The Beeching Era)

Nationalization was the main event of the 1940s, but underlying trends in the railway industry had not halted. Investment was too low, and by the 1950s the industry had made little progress from its 'golden ages' earlier in the century. The challenge of road transport had been joined by the airways, and steam technology now seemed anachronistic. In other countries, diesel and electrification were challenging the steam status quo: politically, the argument was to favour steam (using domestic coal, also a national-ized industry) over diesel, which had to be imported (until the North Sea discoveries in the 1960s).

The mid-1950s brought an official modernization plan for British Rail, but this proved insufficient to handle mounting deficits, leading to rationaliza-tion in the 1960s. (Some rail historians have argued that, had modernization been more suitable, the later cuts in services would not have been neces-sary.) *The Reshaping of British Railways*, authored by Dr Richard Beeching, Chairman of British Rail, was published in 1963, with Draconian recom-mendations for line and station closures, leading to 'Beeching' becoming a byword for rationalization, whether as a prefix for 'cuts' or 'the axe'.

The 'Beeching axe' removed nine lines in the Highlands, together with dozens of stations and passenger services. Across Britain, one-third of stations and over 5,000 route miles were deemed uneconomic, and closed.

The Beeching 'axe' could have been much sharper in Scotland but for lobbying against closures within the Highlands. Credit for saving northern High-land railway lines was due to Frank Spaven (1917–2003) whose son, David, became an equally ardent campaigner for rail and a prolific author on the subject (his books include *Highland Survivor* and *The Railway Atlas of Scotland*).

Two victims of change: BR 60019 Bittern *hauling the 'A4 Farewell Tour' of 1966 at Forfar station (closed in 1967 under Beeching).*
JOHN ROBIN, 1966

Fin De Siécle: **The Move Towards Reprivatization**

The 1960s are obviously remembered for 'Beeching' rationalization, but the Labour governments (1964–70) did recognize that some railway lines were 'socially and economically desirable' and therefore worthy of subsidy even if they were loss-making.

Technology dominated the 1970s, with the completed move from steam to diesel or electric traction, and the launch – in England – of the first 'high speed trains', bringing 'HST' into railway parlance. The term 'InterCity' was coined for the first of these and is still used in Scotland, albeit adapted as Inter7City for connecting seven cities – Edinburgh, Glasgow, Stirling, Dundee, Perth, Aberdeen and Inverness – using sets that, in part, date back to the 1970s.

The 1980s brought the focus back from technology to running the railways as a business in line with Conservative policy under Margaret Thatcher. British Rail operations were classified by business sector – InterCity, commuter services, freight, and so on – rather than by region, and this also meant separating off the engineering division (which foretold later changes under EU law). In terms of hardware, the 'Sprinter' DMU classes were introduced and would have a long-term future on Scottish regional railways.

Privatization of government assets was the main political feature of the 1980s under the Conservatives, although rail would be among the last to shift to the private sector. British Aerospace and British Airways, Cable & Wireless and British Telecom, together with most energy production authorities, were privatized.

By 1990, the scene was set for British Rail to be privatized, and that event, together with the first European regulation 'package' of 1991, would have such a long-lasting impact that it will be discussed in the next chapter, covering the twenty-first century to date (2020). But before leaving the twentieth century behind, some other influential changes of its latter decades may be recalled:

- ScotRail was introduced as the railways brand in Scotland (for the BR Scottish Region) in 1983, pushed through by divisional director Chris Green. BR livery was modified to incorporate the Scottish flag (the saltire). Notably, this happened years before either privatization or Scottish devolution were under discussion
- The opening of the Channel Tunnel brought great publicity for modern railways, albeit a long way from the Highlands. 'Eurostar' for passengers and 'Le Shuttle' for vehicles arrived in the lexicon of modern railways
- British Rail was slimmed down by selling off non-rail subsidiaries involved in station hotels (British Transport Hotels), shipping and catering. As the previous chapters of this book have mentioned, good quality station hotels were once seen as an integral part of the railway offer in Scottish cities and towns, and Scottish rail companies also had a particularly close relationship with shipping (for passenger ferries and freight) in their early history

CHAPTER 9

Scottish Highland Railways in the Twenty-First Century

Notwithstanding its title, this chapter takes up the story of railways in Scotland from 1990 onwards, as a more logical approach to describing the modern era of privatized services (under 'franchises') and political devolution.

ScotRail in the UK, and EU Regulation to 2019

'ScotRail' was coined as a brand in 1984 (for BR's Scottish region) but would become a more totemic symbol of the railways in Scotland after devolution. However, ScotRail must still be considered in the context of both UK and EU legislation and regulation.

Under the Conservative governments of the 1980s, privatization was introduced at many former government 'departments', but it was the European railway 'package' of 1991 (EU Directive 91/440) that opened the door to rail privatization. The 1991 directive – only the first of several legislation 'packages' – ruled that separate bodies must manage the 'infrastructure' and the 'transport operations' in EU member states. The UK's Railways Act of 1993 went further towards privatization than was the case in other EU countries. The infrastructure role was taken on privately by Railtrack – later renationalized in 2014 as Network Rail – while various private companies ('train operating companies', or TOCs) took on the regional franchises for passenger services.

The Scottish region of British Rail, already branded as ScotRail, was offered as a single franchise; the first winner was National Express, originally a UK bus and coach operator. From 2004 to 2015, FirstGroup (based in Aberdeen) held the franchise, and was then superseded by Abellio, which won the franchise (to 2021 or later) against bids from the two previous franchises and from Arriva, a leading transport franchise in England.

Abellio is part of the Dutch group of that name, which is ultimately controlled by the Netherlands government (as Nederlands Spoorwegen). Abellio ScotRail is the name of the TOC, but the branding as ScotRail has been made permanent by the Scottish government.

While ScotRail operates as the internal TOC for Scotland, four other UK franchises run trains into the country:

InterCity East Coast: A franchise held since June 2018 by LNER (London North Eastern Railway), a 'nationalized' service controlled by the UK Department of Transport. The service extends from England through Edinburgh to Aberdeen and Inverness.

InterCity West Coast: (Terminates in Glasgow.) From December 2019, a franchise operated by West Coast Partnership (70 per cent owned by FirstGroup, 30 per cent by Trenitalia), formerly by Virgin Trains (which also operated the East Coast line until 2018).

New CrossCountry: Operated by Arriva (owned by Deutsche Bahn) – a route from southern England that terminates in Aberdeen.

Caledonian Sleeper: Operated by Serco – overnight 'hotel trains' from London to five Scottish cities.

Ever since their debut as a form of transport, railways have had to respond to government regulation; the Railway Regulation Act (1840) started the ball rolling, forcing companies to comply with Board of Trade rules and provide the Board with financial returns. (The authors of the Act also found it necessary to stipulate the 'prohibition of drunkenness by railway employees'.)

Appendix V provides more detail on current regulatory bodies affecting the railways in Scotland.

After 2020: The Future of ScotRail

This book was completed at a time of change and uncertainty for the future of railways in Scotland. Decisions were pending on the future franchise for ScotRail, on the UK-wide Williams Review of rail, and, at a broader level, on Scottish participation – as part of the UK – in the European Union.

Conclusions on the future had to be tentative, therefore, but there are some underlying, undeniable changes and demands that the future will bring for Scottish Highland railways. Some recent positives and negatives will be reviewed – many of which have always been part of railway culture and criticism – but the focus is on the long-term need to attract young people and foreign visitors to railway travel at a time of great change in human communications and attitudes towards the public transport system.

Future Issue 1: Service Criticism

Hello ScotRail – I can't make your public meeting tonight at 7pm in Kirkcaldy where you intend to take questions on the appalling services in Fife because you've cancelled the rush hour Kirkcaldy train.

Tweet reported by edinburghlive.co.uk
on 1 March 2019

In 2019, Abellio ScotRail held a series of 'public meetings' where company representatives answered questions about recent problems on the network, particularly affecting suburban commuter services. There were some angry exchanges. In a Scottish Parliament debate in April, the First Minister, Nicola Sturgeon, declared that the Abellio franchise was 'in the last chance saloon', following the release of statistics showing that the company had missed its targets for punctuality, and that customer satisfaction with Scottish railways had fallen to its lowest for sixteen years. Abellio itself claimed that:

We're building the best railway Scotland has ever had. The investment we are making now will transform Scotland's railway for years to come. We're introducing brand new electric trains, recreating an InterCity network with our high-speed trains, and upgrading many of our existing trains to make them as good as new. This will mean more seats, faster journeys and even better services. We are also upgrading our stations, rolling out our queue-busting Smartcard, and transforming how we get information to our customers.

So the good news in the 2018–2020 period was that the ScotRail franchise holder was taking its part in some deep underlying changes affecting rail across Britain as a whole. In April 2018, *Rail Engineer* magazine analysed the changes ahead for British railways – particularly stemming from electrification – and suggested that, with more than 50 per cent of the passenger rolling stock being replaced, 'Britain's trains are about to change as never before'.

In this transitional period, ScotRail faced the problem of retraining staff for electrification, while requiring them to continue working the existing stock and timetables – and the late delivery of two new fleets did not help. Some unusual weather conditions were also unhelpful, although, as always, the media were waiting to pounce: phrases such as 'leaves on the line' and 'the wrong type of snow' have been used to ridicule the railway service in the past. (In 1991, UK media seized on a British Rail television interview in which the interviewer coined the phrase 'wrong type of snow' after the BR executive had explained the problems with the recent heavy, melting snow. The ensuing ridicule echoed a previous mocking of a 'leaves on the line' explanation, although both autumn leaf fall and heavy snow have always been hazardous to safe railway operations.)

Future Issue 2: Political Control

Criticism of the railways by the media, politicians and consumers is hardly new: it dates back to the very origins of rail in Britain as a public transport system that has variously been operated by private companies, government departments, or a mixture of the two. The apparently disparate factors affecting the railways are, in fact, interconnected – and they always have been. Ownership and control, media coverage, safety, even environmental concerns were tangled up back in the nineteenth century.

The hoariest old chestnut in railway history has been revived: nationalization of the country's rail system, advocated by more than one political party, including the Scottish National Party. Proponents argue for public ownership of public transport to ensure maximum investment in the service, while opponents, in favour of private input, point to the danger of a state-employed workforce 'holding the government to ransom' on an essential public service.

In practice, a country's railway system will always depend on some public input. As pointed out by David Ross in his comprehensive 2017 review *Getting the Train*, ScotRail is already subsidized 'to the tune of £700 million a year, or £140 for every man, woman and child in Scotland', despite the perception of ScotRail being entirely run by a private – and foreign controlled – franchisor.

Future Issue 3: Pricing

Despite the regular resurrection of old criticisms, arguments and opinions, some changes affecting rail are new. In particular, there is the way rail journeys are priced. A common criticism – especially by older rail users – is the complex variation in rail fares for journeys of similar length, depending on time of travel, route taken, date of booking and other factors.

Getting the pricing right is clearly essential if the underlying economic/environmental aim is to 'take traffic off the roads'. But the new generation of rail users is fully acquainted with the concept of dynamic pricing, driven by on-line commerce and the need to plan ahead for the best deals.

Users of the excellent website, The Man in Seat 61 (created by Mark Smith), have long known that dynamic pricing for individual journeys will offer far better deals than, for example, discount passes such as BritRail (or ScotRail's Highland Rover). For modern consumers, this dovetails with dynamic pricing on airlines and even bus routes, as well as the choice afforded by on-line shopping for almost everything.

Future Issue 4: The Digital Era

'What is wrong with you people?!' shouted actor Martin Freeman as he stomped angrily down a crowded railway carriage full of passengers who were all staring at their computers or phones (plus a guard, seen lurking in the WC). Freeman was playing the frustrated, older passenger hoping to have a conversation with a stranger during his journey, but who is thwarted by modern technology.

The 2019 commercial was for Vodafone, a mobile phone company, but the subtext was that train travel can be ultra-modern in that it can offer strong enough wi-fi to watch a movie or television programme, or listen to streamed music. As a national railway company, ScotRail is having to adapt to the demands created by modern technology while at the same time bringing in other elements of twenty-first century travel.

Some Other Future Issues

Dynamic pricing for booking online and good wi-fi are just two of the future issues to be faced by any ScotRail franchise, but society also demands much more. There are, for example, ever more stringent safety requirements, and demands for inclusiveness for all types of passengers; also for reduced pollution; and for more passenger space: for buggies, bicycles, wheelchairs and just the extra luggage carried by tourists (especially on Highland lines). Stations are expected to provide ample racks for cyclists and perhaps a rent-a-bike scheme, which neatly dovetails two 'green' forms of transport – modern electric trains and cycling.

Disabilities have to be catered for, from wheelchair ramps and low-floor carriages to braille signage and accessible toilets. It was a ten-year-old Scottish girl, Grace Warnock, who started the campaign to allow people with 'invisible disabilities' – such as Crohn's disease, which she suffers – to use accessible public toilets. Grace's sign reads 'Not every disability is visible': it is now seen widely across Scotland, but it started at railway stations.

The modern spirit of inclusiveness is even recognized by priority seating on ScotRail trains, the upholstery designed with cartoons of passengers who are pregnant, with infants or who have a mobility issue.

Another necessity for making train travel appeal to the latest generation is a high standard of catering, whether at the station or on the train. The coffee shop explosion alone has forced the railways to adjust to modern tastes, whether from on-board trolleys or coffee 'pods' in stations. Things have certainly moved on from the infamous 'British Rail sandwich' of old (!) although the traditional, cosy tearoom is still a welcome feature at some Highland stations.

Recognizing the interest in food, ScotRail's Great Scenic Tasting Box was offered for sale to passengers departing from Glasgow Queen Street or Inverness, the box containing a mixture of 'tasty Scottish delights' such as oatcakes, charcuterie and shortbread for passengers to enjoy 'while the stunning scenery passes by'.

Hogwarts Express: The New Legacy?

Harry: Excuse me, sir. Can you tell me where I might find Platform 9¾?
Trainmaster: 9¾? Think ya being funny, do ya? (Leaves)

Film script of Harry Potter and the
Philosopher's Stone

It is a fair bet that millions of the eager young fans who watched this scene from the first Harry Potter movie had never experienced a railway station of the Victorian era. Later in the movie, train travel was made to seem thrilling by the use of a steam locomotive (*The Jacobite*, en route to Mallaig) as the fictional Hogwarts Express train taking Harry and his young colleagues to their school for young wizards, with a memorable crossing of the Glenfinnan Viaduct.

Passengers at Glenfinnan station have doubled over ten years, and indications are that the demand will continue to rise. The heritage service between Fort William and Mallaig used locomotive no. 5972 *Olton Hall* (a 4-6-0 Hall Class built in 1937) for the filming, and the engine was later displayed at 'The Making of Harry Potter', a studio theme park run by Warner Brothers near London. There are replicas on display at other Potter-themed attractions in Florida and Japan, all driving up awareness of the allure of train travel for a new generation.

Railway heritage appears to be of growing interest to a younger generation, marking a refreshing difference from the sardonic use of the title *Trainspotting* in the 1990s for Irvine Welsh's phenomenally successful youth-oriented book and the subsequent movie. Equally refreshing has been the success and publicity for Vicki Pipe and Geoff Marshall, the two young authors of *The Railway Adventures*; the book was based on their unusual YouTube channel, All The Stations, which showed them attempting to travel through all 2,563 British railway stations in

2017. By 2019, the YouTube channel had over 50,000 subscribers.

On top of the media coverage, new generations are being attracted to rail by their parallel fascination with outdoor pursuits (or 'extreme sports') and environmental concerns. Trains through the Highlands are convenient for reaching remote areas for walking, climbing and camping, and the 'green' credentials of public transport are familiar enough. The Glasgow to Fort William run, for example, opens up the chance to climb Britain's highest peak, Ben Nevis, or take the Nevis resort's funicular up the mountain and cycle down. (The Nevis range has regularly hosted mountain biking World Cups.) Or simply escaping the crowds on remote, lonely railway lines has a growing appeal.

Stations and the Local Community

Another reason to feel confident in the future of Scottish Highland railways, despite the stumbling

Bookshop at Pitlochry station: well stocked and serving hot drinks. 'Every penny to charity'.

blocks that every phase of railway history brings, is the care that voluntary groups are expressing in looking after their local stations as assets to the community.

Encouraged by the UK government and supported by the UK national Association of Community Rail Partnerships (ACoRP, based in Huddersfield), local people have been involved in 'adopting' Scottish stations since 2005, and since 2012 the Scottish Government has provided funding for Community Rail Partnerships (CRPs) with the aim of uniting rail services with local towns.

There has also been a proliferation of stations old and new taking part in Scottish Highland tourism by being converted, in one way or another, into holiday accommodation: each journey chapter of this book offered illustrations of this, ranging from modest hostel dormitories for back-packers up to premium-priced apartments and houses for families and couples.

2020 and Beyond

At the time this was written, the new decade starting in 2020 appeared to hold more uncertainties than certainties in terms of the future of railways in the Scottish Highlands, within the broader context of rail in Scotland as a whole, and in the United Kingdom. To this political uncertainty was added the unpredictable impact, both short- and long-term, of the global coronavirus epidemic that began in 2019 (*see* Preface).

During 2019, the industry awaited the promised 'root and branch' Williams Review into the future of the UK network, with an interim report (in July) focusing on four key areas: an improved 'passenger offer'; 'simplified fares and ticketing' – taking cues from the airline industry; 'better aligning of track and train'; and 'a new commercial model':

> What's absolutely clear is that the current franchising model has had its day.
>
> Keith Williams, Chair, Williams Review
> interim report, 16 July 2019

(Keith Williams was a former chief executive of British Airways and was appointed chairman at Royal Mail in 2019. The review was due to be published in autumn 2019, but publication was later delayed until 2020.)

At the time of writing, therefore, this author was inhibited from drawing firm conclusions by the future uncertainties, not only over the status of Abellio, but of deeper issues, such as the UK's relationship with the European Union (with a potential impact on railway legislation) and even Scotland's long-term place within the United Kingdom. (Irrespective of calls for a second referendum on Scottish independence, the Scotland Act of 2016 granted the Scottish government the right to bid for the ScotRail franchise, which might mean a partial return to a 'nationalized' service in Scotland.)

Some positive points can be left as conclusions, however, in terms of the grass-roots impact on Scottish Highland railways in the near future:

- Abellio has invested in major modernization projects such as introducing HST on the Highland Main Line, and doubling the track on Aberdeen–Inverness: in a nutshell, faster and more frequent services
- Improvements and modernization at most Highland stations have been very visible, and station reopenings have replaced the legacy of stations being closed
- The upgraded Caledonian Sleeper – operated under franchise by Serco, not by ScotRail – went into service in 2019, improving the image of an iconic, historic railway journey from London to the Highlands
- In 2019, LNER introduced its 'revolutionary' Azuma multiple units (bi-modal: diesel and electric traction, made by Hitachi) on the lines from London to Aberdeen and Inverness

Observers of Scottish rail should also note that the discontent described at the beginning of this chapter was targeted mainly at commuter services in the Central Belt, rather than Highland lines – the beneficiaries of an undeniable increase in the appeal

At Taynuilt station on the way to Oban, stopping for the token while keenly anticipating Highland views beyond the old stone road bridge.

of northern Scotland as a tourist destination. A few examples of this trend will suffice, from a market for inbound tourism to Scotland that has been growing in double percentage figures in recent years:

- More services on Fort William–Mallaig to serve the 'Hogwarts Express' demand – for those who book the Jacobite steam excursion one way and ScotRail to or from Fort William or Mallaig.

Passenger numbers (annual 'entries and exits') at Glenfinnan station were up from 3,536 in 1997/98 to 5,307 in 2007/08, 8,246 in 2012/13 and 11,620 in 2017/18

- Demand for visits to Inverness and various other destinations (particularly Culloden) made famous in the books and television series, *Outlander*. Two newer movies made in 2018 – *Outlaw King* and *Mary Queen of Scots* – have

boosted media-driven tourism to Scotland, albeit partly to the south of the country
- At a gentler level of increase, demand for outdoor pursuits is helping the Highlands raise its international profile among young travellers

Long term, the prospects for the Highland railways will depend on deeper, underlying trends in demand for a rail service. The environmental benefits of public transport are obvious, especially in a country moving towards eradicating its 'carbon footprint': by the end of 2019, over three-quarters of Scottish electricity consumption, for example, already came from renewable sources.

Allied to 'green' concerns among younger travellers is a desire to experience the countryside without being behind the wheel of a car, so train travel dovetails with the 'great outdoors' trend. It may be a truism, but the future does lie with the young, and there are encouraging signs that the millennial generation may become as keen on train travel as their baby-boomer grandparents.

The most positive news of all is that of 'reversing' the twentieth-century closure of lines and stations, and even opening new ones. In 2019, the Conservative party manifesto – prior to the party winning the general election in December – even included a pledge to create a 'Beeching Reversal Fund' worth £500m to British railways. Whatever the outcome of this, the pledge draws attention to railway investment. As noted in this book, several new (or usually revived) stations in the Highlands have been successful beyond the anticipated passenger traffic. In the south of the country, a Borders line was reopened, and the journey connecting Alloa to Stirling (thence Glasgow and Edinburgh) was reinstated after exactly forty years of closure (1968–2008). The Stirling–Alloa branch quickly welcomed over 400,000 passengers a year, against the forecast of 155,000.

Stations Open in 2020[*]

East Coast (Chapter 2)
(Edinburgh–Leuchars–Dundee)
Broughty Ferry
Balmossie
Monifieth
Barry Links
Golf Street
Carnoustie
Arbroath
Montrose
Laurencekirk
Stonehaven
Portlethen
Aberdeen

Aberdeen–Inverness (Chapter 3)
Dyce
Inverurie
Insch
Huntly
Keith
Elgin
Forres
Nairn
Inverness

Main Line (Chapter 4)
(Glasgow Queen Street–Stirling–Dunblane–Perth)
Dunkeld & Birnam
Pitlochry
Blair Atholl
Dalwhinnie
Newtonmore
Kingussie
Aviemore
Carrbridge
Inverness

Far North (Chapter 5)
Inverness–Dingwall (*see* Chapter 7 Kyle Line)
Alness
Invergordon
Fearn
Tain
Ardgay
Culrain
Invershin
Lairg
Rogart
Golspie
Dunrobin Castle
Brora
Helmsdale
Kildonan

Kinbrace
Forsinard
Altnabreac
Scotscalder
Georgemas Junction
Thurso/Wick

West Highland (Chapter 6)
(Glasgow Queen Street–Dalmuir–Dumbarton
    Central)
Helensburgh Upper
Garelochhead
Arrochar & Tarbet
Ardlui
Crianlarich (junction)
Upper Tyndrum
Bridge of Orchy
Rannoch
Corrour
Tulloch
Roy Bridge
Spean Bridge
Fort William

Oban extension (Chapter 7)
(Crianlarich; and *see* West Highland)
Tyndrum Lower
Dalmally
Loch Awe
Falls of Cruachan
Taynuilt
Connel Ferry

Oban
Mallaig extension (Chapter 7)
(Fort William; and *see* West Highland)
Banavie
Corpach
Loch Eil Outward
Locheilside
Glenfinnan
Lochailort
Beasdale
Arisaig
Morar
Mallaig

Kyle Line (Chapter 7)
Inverness
Beauly
Muir of Ord
Conon Bridge
Dingwall (junction)
Garve
Lochluichart
Achanalt
Achnasheen
Achnashellach
Strathcarron
Attadale
Stromeferry
Duncraig
Plockton
Duirinish
Kyle of Lochalsh

---

* Stations within the Scottish Highlands as defined in Chapter 1

Company Family Tree

The chart below shows history in reverse, starting with the current franchise situation for ScotRail (the main passenger train franchisee in Scotland), back through the public ownership phase (BR Scottish Region) to the 'grouping' of 1921, when two of the UK 'big four' – LMS and LNER – had Scottish operations. The table shows the companies that constituted these two (for example, Caledonian and Highland, in LMS) and some earlier companies that had amalgamated into these (for example, Aberdeen Railway into SNER).

ScotRail – passenger franchises since 1997
    Abellio 2015–
    FirstGroup 2004–2015
    National Express 1997–2004

British Rail – Scottish Region (1948–1997) ('ScotRail' from 1983)

'Big Four' after grouping 1921–1948[1]

  LMS (London Midland & Scottish)[2]
    Caledonian Railway
      Scottish Central Railway[3]
      Scottish North Eastern Railway
        Aberdeen Railway
        Scottish Midland Junction Railway[4]

    Highland Railway
      Inverness & Aberdeen Junction Railway
      Inverness & Perth Junction Railway
      Inverness & Ross-shire Railway[5]
      Sutherland & Caithness[6] (Far North)

  LNER (London & North Eastern Railway)[7]
    North British Railway
      West Highland Railway
      Invergarry & Fort Augustus
    Great North of Scotland Railway
      Formantine & Buchan Railway
      Morayshire Railway
      Alford Valley Railway
      Banff Macduff & Turriff Railways
      Keith & Dufftown Railway
      Strathspey Railway
      Deeside Railway

[1] UK rail companies were forced into four groups, of which Great Western and Southern only operated in England and Wales.
[2] LMS also took over Glasgow & South Western in Scotland and five English companies.
[3] SCR had absorbed Dundee & Perth, Dunblane Doune & Callander (and Callander & Oban) and Crieff Junction.
[4] SMJR's main line was from Perth to Forfar.

[5] Forerunner of the Kyle Line (Inverness–Kyle of Lochalsh).

[6] Forerunner of the Far North Line (Inverness–Thurso/Wick).

[7] Also contained four English companies including Great Eastern and Great Northern. The LNER name and brand was revived in 2018 as the new East Coast franchise, taking over from Virgin Trains.

Source: Author

Timeline of Highland Railway Companies

The early corporate history of railways in the Highlands was exceedingly complex, with differing dates attached to lines being proposed, given parliamentary approval (and royal assent), ceremonial 'cutting of the first sod' through to official opening days. Subsequent timelines are littered with working and timetable agreements, amalgamations or line failures. To simplify this, the timeline below shows a selection of dates for line openings, usually to passenger traffic. Many lines started initially for freight only, and in the twentieth century many closed to passengers before closing to freight and then completely. The largest companies, with their abbreviations, are in bold type.

1831	Dundee & Newtyle
1838	Dundee & Arbroath
1839	Arbroath & Forfar
1847	Aberdeen Railway
1847	Dundee & Perth
1851	Morayshire Railway
1853	Deeside Railway (to Banchory)
1854	**Great North of Scotland Railway (GNOS):** Aberdeen (Kittybrewster) to Huntly; extended to Keith in 1856
1855	Inverness & Nairn
1856	Scottish North Eastern Railway (SNER) amalgamates Aberdeen Railway and Scottish Midland Junction Railway (lines in Angus), later absorbs Dundee & Arbroath and Perth, Almond Valley & Methven. Creates a through journey from Perth to Aberdeen
1856	Perth & Dunkeld, worked by SNER
1856	Crieff Junction Railway
1857	**Inverness & Aberdeen Junction (I&AJ):** Nairn to Forres then Elgin and Keith (1858)
1857	Banff, Macduff & Turriff Junction Railway
1858	I&AJ absorbs Inverness & Nairn
1858	Dunblane, Doune & Callander (worked by Scottish Central Railway)
1859	Banff Portsoy & Strathisla

1859	Deeside extended to Aboyne
1860	Findhorn Railway to Kinloss
1861	Main line: assent granted for Dunkeld to Forres
1861	GNOS: Formantine & Buchan (serving Dyce, Peterhead, Fraserburgh, Ellon)
1862	Inverness & Ross-shire (Inverness–Dingwall), line immediately absorbed by I&AJ
1862	Keith & Dufftown
1862	Alves–Hopeman Branch
1863	I&AJ: Inverness–Dingwall extended to Invergordon (start of Far North)
1863	Strathspey Railway (Dufftown–Abernethy, later named Nethy Bridge)
1863	**Inverness & Perth Junction (I&PJ)** launched: absorbs Perth & Dunkeld
1865	**Highland Railway (HR) formed from I&AJ and I&PJ**
1865	Aberfeldy–Ballinluig (HR)
1866	Deeside extended to Ballater
1866/1867	**GNOS absorbs most Grampian lines (Deeside in 1876)**
1866	SNER absorbed by **Caledonian Railway**
1866	Crieff & Methven Junction (joins Perth line)
1868	Sutherland Railway (Bonar Bridge–Golspie)
1870	Duke of Sutherland's Railway (Helmsdale–Dunrobin [private], extended to Golspie 1871)
1870	Dingwall & Skye (Dingwall–Stromeferry)
1870	**Callander & Oban (C&O):** Callander–Glenoglehead, branch to Killin. Later extended to Tyndrum (1873), Dalmally (1877), Oban (1880)
1874	Sutherland & Caithness (financed HR and Duke of Sutherland): Helmsdale to Thurso/ Wick
1880	HR absorbs Dingwall & Skye
1881	GNOS absorbs Morayshire
1881	**North British Railway (NBR)** absorbs Montrose & Bervie
1884	HR's Inverness & Aviemore Direct given assent
1884	Sutherland & Caithness and Duke of Sutherland's absorbed by HR
1884	GNOS Moray Coast: Portsoy–Tochieneal–Garmouth (1885)
1885	Strathpeffer Branch (HR) from Dingwall–Skye
1892	HR Aviemore 'Direct': Aviemore–Carrbridge
1893	Crieff & Comrie
1893	Fochabers Branch (HR) from Orbliston Junction
1894	**West Highland Line (WHL)**
1894	Black Isle Railway (HR): Muir of Ord–Fortrose
1897	Dingwall & Skye (HR) extended from Stromeferry–Kyle of Lochalsh
1897	HR Aviemore 'Direct' extended from Carrbridge to Daviot
1897	Lochearnhead (Balquidder Junction) via St Fillans to Comrie
1898	HR Aviemore 'Direct' reaches Inverness (from Daviot)
1899	Fort George Branch (HR)
1899	GNOS: Boddam–Ellon–Cruden Bay Hotel
1901	WHL: extended Fort William (Banavie) to Mallaig
1902	Dornoch Light Railway
1903	GNOS: Fraserburgh–St Combs
1903	Invergarry & Fort Augustus (operated by HR, then NRB – final owner)
1903	C&O: Ballachulish Branch

Station Usage: Examples of Passenger 'Entries and Exits', 2018–19

Edinburgh	Scottish capital	23,872,996
Aberdeen	Busiest station in Highlands	2,616,142
Dundee	Major East Coast station	2,015,782
Inverness	Junction for four lines	1,243,338
Oban	West Highland terminus; ferry port	177,522
Aviemore	Highlands 'playground'	138,490
Fort William	West Highland terminus + junction	160,418
Keith	Busy commercial town midway Inverness/Aberdeen	81,112
Kyle of Lochalsh	Terminus of Kyle line/gateway to Isle of Skye	60,606
Beauly	Commuter town for Inverness; tourist appeal	48,270
Thurso	Terminus of Far North/ferry to Orkney	39,974
Blair Atholl	Main Line station, access to Blair Castle	21,008
Crianlarich	Junction on West Highland; crossroads town	16,960
Arrochar & Tarbet	Crossroads station; near Loch Lomond	20,192
Wick	Terminus of Far North	17,890
Plockton*	Popular resort town on Kyle line	11,482
Rannoch	Remote moorland station on West Highland	8,834
Bridge of Orchy	Accommodation/walkers' stop on West Highland	6,490
Dalwhinnie	Little-used Main Line station; many distillery visitors	3,368
Achnasheen	Rare crossroads in the North-West Highlands	3,284
Dunrobin Castle	Purpose-built for Castle visitors; seasonal	1,224
Achnashellach	Request station on Kyle line	820
Falls of Cruachan	Seasonal station (summer) on Oban line	538
Invershin	Request station on Far North	284
Beasdale	Request station on Mallaig line	342
Duncraig	Former private station still within Castle grounds	484
Barry Links	Least used station in Britain 2017–18	122

* includes substantial usage by Plockton High School students

Source: Office of Rail and Road

Rail Organizations and Regulation in Scotland

Since 1997, privatization of the network and devolution of government in Scotland have made regulation even more complex. Under the Scotland Act (1998), Scotland gained more influence over its transport than it had before but the UK government reserved powers for some aspects of transport including aviation, maritime policy and 'strategic' road and rail. The last of these reserved powers cover rail safety and regulation including rail accident prevention and investigation and technical standards relating to the transport of disabled people.

Transport Scotland, the executive agency for transport issues in Scotland, regulates rail as one of six transport directorates working through regional partnerships, whose boards are comprised of representative councillors from local authorities. There are two for the Highlands: HITRANS (Highlands & Islands Transport Partnership) and NESTRANS for the North East, based in Aberdeen.

The Office of Rail and Road (ORR) has UK-wide powers to regulate and monitor the railways (and roads, in England), while the Rail Delivery Group (RDG) is an umbrella trade association for Abellio and other TOCs, Network Rail and other private companies operating on British rail networks. RDG also runs national rail enquiries, and markets cross-franchise products such as railcards.

In 2015, Network Rail and Abellio created a managerial partnership called ScotRail Alliance, which manages over 350 stations and 3,000 miles of track, employs 7,000 railway staff and runs more than 2,500 train services daily.

As part of the UK, Scotland has been obliged to abide by European Union legislation; over the years, the Union has adopted a number of legislative packages governing rail in EU member states. At the time of writing, the UK was negotiating withdrawal from the Union, with no clarity on which EU regulations covering transport would be preserved.

RAIL ORGANIZATIONS AND REGULATION IN SCOTLAND

Abellio ScotRail	Franchisee (passenger services)
ScotRail Alliance	ScotRail + Network Rail (UK infrastructure)
Rail Delivery Group	Joint industry representation (UK)
Transport Scotland	Scottish government agency
HITRANS/NESTRANS	Regional partnerships
Network Rail	UK infrastructure owner (public)
Office of Rail and Road	UK regulatory office
EU Railway Agency (ERA)	European Union railways agency

Sources

There is now a formidable array of books available on the history of British and Scottish railways and the author acknowledges these, together with the modern addition of information from a proliferating number of railway magazines, internet websites, television programmes and videos (as DVDs or on YouTube). It has also been enjoyable and instructive to refer to previous 'classics' such as *The North of Scotland* (by John Thomas and David Turnock), part of an encylopaedic regional British series published in the 1980s, and even W.M. Acworth's seminal 1890 volume on *The Railways of Scotland*.

This book draws on many of these publications, and there is a Sources section at the end of each specific 'journey' chapter. Special acknowledgements, however, should go to the following:

- Staff at the Scottish Railway Preservation Society (SRPS), including its Museum of Scottish Railways, for the provision of archive material, particularly Ailsa Hutton, Assistant Curator
- Staff at the National Records of Scotland, which holds 'the largest written and pictorial archive of Scottish railway history'
- RailScot (www.railscot.co.uk), called 'a history of railways with an emphasis on Scottish railways'. Supplied by over 320 contributors, the site holds over 60,000 photographs but also has written descriptions of operators, stations, signal boxes and so on, and an efficient search engine

Books

Specific: Highland Railways

Thomas, J. and Turnock, D., *A Regional History of the Railways of Great Britain Vol. 15: The North of Scotland* (David & Charles 1989)

Note: Scottish author John Thomas passed away while writing this book, but David Turnock completed it, incorporating 'nearly all of the original work' by John Thomas

The History of the Railways of the Scottish Highlands (series 1977–1990):
Originally published by David & Charles, now from House of Lochar, Isle of Colonsay:

Thomas, J., *The West Highland Railway*

Vallance, H.A., *The Highland Railway*

Vallance, H.A., *The Great North of Scotland Railway*

Thomas, J., *The Callander & Oban Railway*

Thomas, J., *The Skye Railway* (Inverness–Kyle line)

Great North of Scotland Railway Association (publisher):

Fenwick, K., Flett, D. and Jackson, D., *Railways of Buchan* (2008)

Jackson, D., *Rails to Alford: Story of the Railway from Kintore to Alford* (2006)

Jackson, D., *Royal Deeside's Railway: Aberdeen to Ballater* (1999)

Jackson, D., *The Speyside Line: The Railway from Craigellachie to Boat of Garten* (2006)

Jones, K. G., *The Railways of Aberdeen: 150 Years of History* (2000)

Northern Books from Famedram Publishers:

The Rannoch Line (1983)

The Kyle Line in Pictures (2005)

The Mallaig Railway (2009)

The Story of the West Highland: The 1940s LNER Guide (2001; reprint)

Rails Across Rannoch (2013)

Scotland's Stations: A Traveller's Guide (2017)

Burgess, R. and Kinghorn, R., *Moray Coast Railways* (Mercat Press 1989)

Christopher, J. and McCutcheon, C., *Locomotives of the Highland Railway* (Amberley 2014)

Crawford, E., *Callander & Oban Railway Through Time* (Amberley 2013)

Fenwick, K., *The Highland Railway (Britain in Old Photographs)* (The History Press 2009)

Fenwick, K. and Sinclair N. T., *Lost Stations on the Far North Line: The Impact of the Railway Closures North of Inverness in 1960* (Highland Railway Society 2010)

Hogg, C. and Patrick, L., *Scottish Railway Icons: The Highlands* (Amberley 2019)

Holland, J., *Discovering Scotland's Lost Railways* (Waverley Books 2009)

Kennedy, D., *The Birth and Death of a Highland Railway: The Ballachulish Line* (John Murray 1971)

Kernahan, J., *The Black Isle Railway* (Highland Railway Society 2013)

McConnell, D., *Rails to Wick & Thurso* (Dornoch 1989)

McConnell, D., *Rails to Kyle of Lochalsh* (Oakwood Press 1997)

McGregor, J., *The West Highland Line: Great Railway Journeys Through Time* (Amberley 2013)

Miller, J., *The Finest Road in the World: The Story of Travel and Transport in the Scottish Highlands* (Birlinn 2017)

Paterson, Anne-Mary, *Spanning the Gaps: Highland railway bridges and viaducts* (Highland Railway Society 2017)

Pearson, M., *Iron Road to the Isles: A Travellers and Tourist Guide to the West Highland Line* (J.M. Pearson & Sons 2001)

Price, D., *The Kyle of Lochalsh and Far North Lines* (Amberley 2018)

Ross, D., *The Highland Railway* (Stenlake 2005)

Simms, W., *Railways of Mull and Iona* (Wilfred F. Simms 2001)

Sinclair, N., *The Highland Main Line* (Atlantic Transport 1998)

Sinclair, N., *Highland Railway: People and Places* (Breedon Books 2005)

Spaven, D., *Highland Survivor: The Story of the Far North Line* (Kessock Books 2016)

Stansfield, G., *Banff, Moray and Nairn's Lost Railways* (Stenlake 2000)

Tatlow, P., *A History of Highland Locomotives* (OPC Railprint 1989)

Victorian Travel on the West Highland Line: By Mountain, Moor and Loch in 1894 (House of Lochar 2002)

Wham, A., *Trossachs and West Highlands: Exploring the Lost Railways* (Stenlake 2009)

General: Scottish or British Railways

Acworth, W.M., *The Railways of Scotland* (John Murray 1890)

Jackson, J., *The Scottish Rail Scene in the Twenty-First Century* (Amberley 2019)

Nock, O.S., *Scottish Railways* (Thomas Nelson 1950)

Nock, O.S., *The Railway Enthusiast's Encylopedia* (Hutchinson & Co 1968)

Ransom, P.J.G., *Iron Road – The Railway in Scotland* (Birlinn 2007)

Ross, D., *Getting the Train: The History of Scotland's Railways* (Stenlake 2018)

Ross, D., *Scottish Railways 1923–2016 – A History* (Stenlake 2018)

St John Thomas, D. and Whitehouse, P., *The Romance of Scotland's Railways* (Atlantic Transport Publishers 1993)

Simmons, J. (Ed) and Biddle, G. (Ed) *The Oxford Companion to British Railway History: From 1603 to the 1990s* (OUP 1997)

Spaven, D., *The Railway Atlas of Scotland: Two Hundred Years of History in Maps* (Birlinn 2018)

Thomas, J., *The Scottish Railway Book* (David & Charles 1977)

Wolmar, C., *Fire and Steam: A New History of the Railways in Britain* (Atlantic Books 2008)

Wolmar, C., *The Iron Road – The Illustrated History of the Railway* (Dorling Kindersley 2014)

Other Railway Topics

Bradshaw's Guides (1863):
    Used as the basis of the TV series, *Great British Railway Journeys* (*see* below, TV and DVD)
    Scotland's Railways – East Coast (McCutcheon, C. and Christopher J.)
    Scotland's Railways – West Coast (Christopher J.)

British Railways Board, *The Reshaping of British Railways 1963* (Collins 2013)

David, G., *Railway Renaissance: Britain's Railways After Beeching* (Pen & Sword Transport 2017)

Engel, M., *Eleven Minutes Late: A Train Journey to the Soul of Britain* (Macmillan 2009)

Fiennes, G., *I Tried to Run a Railway* (Ian Allan 1967)

Hale, D., *Mallard* (Aurum 2005)

Howat, C. J.,
    Diesel Locomotives on Scottish Railways (Amberley 2018)
    Electric Locomotives on Scottish Railways (Amberley 2018)

Martin, M., *Belles and Whistles: Five Journeys Through Time on Britain's Trains* (Profile Books 2015)

Meara, D., *Anglo-Scottish Sleepers* (Amberley Publishing 2018)

Meighan, M., *The Forth Bridges Through Time* (Amberley 2014)

Pipe, V. and Marshall, G., *The Railway Adventures* (September Publishing 2018)

Richards, J. and Mackenzie, J.M., *The Railway Station: A Social History* (OUP 1986)

Simmons, J., *The Victorian Railway* (Thames & Hudson 1991)

Smith, Mark, *The Man in Seat 61* (Bantam 2008)

Smith, Martin, *British Railway Bridges and Viaducts* (Ian Allan 1994)

Other Media

Magazines
Modern Railways (Key Publishing)
Rail (Bauer)
Rail Express (Mortons Media Group)
RailReview (Bauer)
The Railway Magazine (Mortons Media Group)
RTM Rail Technology Magazine (Cognitive Publishing)

TV and DVD Selection
Great British Railway Journeys (BBC Television 2010–14)
   Michael Portillo presents journeys based on the nineteenth-century Bradshaw's guides in five series (115 episodes). Series 2 (2011) episodes 21–25 featured journeys from Ayr through Dumbarton, Tyndrum, Oban, Corrour, Roybridge, Glenfinnan, Lochailort, Mallaig and Skye. **Note:** *Great Railway Journeys of the World* was a 1980 BBC series, one episode featuring London to the Kyle of Lochalsh (*Confessions of a Trainspotter*) presented by Michael Palin (on BBCDVD1626).

Coastal Railways with Julie Walters (Channel 4 2017)
   The actress presents four episodes, the first titled *West Highland Railway*, the second *The East Coast Line (Newcastle to Edinburgh).*

Scottish Railways Remembered (DVD series) (B&R Video Productions – '*recalling the great days of steam on British railways*').

B & R No. 172: *Scottish Railways Remembered* No. 5 DVD (The Highlands) (B&R Video Productions)
Steam in the Hills (Famedram)

Steam to Kyle (Famedram)

The Railway: Keeping Britain on Track (Century Films/BBC Television 2013).
Kevin Whately presented the six-part series including 'North of the Border' (episode 6) set in Scotland.

The World's Most Beautiful Railway (Flint TV 2019)
Six hour-long episodes for Channel 4 about Scottish railways:
1: Union of South Africa, Forth Bridge etc.
2: Flying Scotsman etc.
3: The Jacobite etc.

4: Old Speyside Line etc.

5: Royal Deeside etc.

6: West Highland Line, Waverley and Blair Castle

The Railways of Scotland (CineRail)

Twelve DVDs (running time, 60 minutes) including 4: *Aberdeen and the Grampians*; 5: *The Western Highlands*; 7: *Perth to Kinnaber Junction*; 9: *Routes from Stirling*; and 11: *Edinburgh to Aberdeen*

Internet (www.)

Abellio (Abellio.co.uk)

British Railway Books (britishrailwaybooks.co.uk)

Caledonian Railway (Brechin) (caledonianrailway.co.uk)

Caledonian Sleeper (sleeper.scot)

CrossCountry by Arriva (crosscountrytrains.co.uk)

Friends of the Far North Line (fofnl.org.uk)

Friends of the Kyle Line (kylerailway.co.uk)

Friends of the West Highland Lines (westhighlandline.org.uk)

Great North of Scotland Railway Association (gnsra.org.uk)

Highland Main Line Community Rail Partnership (highlandmainlinecrp.co.uk)

Highland Railway Society (hrsoc.org.uk)

HITRANS: Highlands and Islands Transport Partnership (hitrans.org.uk)

LNER: London North Eastern Railway (lner.co.uk)

NESTRANS: North East Scotland Transport Partnership (nestrans.org.uk)

Network Rail (networkrail.co.uk)

Railfuture Scotland (railfuturescotland.org.uk)

Railnews (railnews.co.uk)

Railscot.co.uk – primary resource for Scottish railway information

Rail UK (railuk.info) – the 'premier UK rail history site'

ScotRail (ScotRail.co.uk) – official website of Abellio franchise

scot-rail (scot-rail.co.uk) – 'Scotland's online rail enthusiast community'

Scottish Railway Preservation Society (srps.org.uk) – operator of excursions (Bo'ness & Kinneil, bkrailway. co.uk) and owner of Museum of Scottish Railways, Bo'ness, West Lothian

Strathspey Railway (strathspeyrailway.co.uk) – Strathspey Railway Association

The Man in Seat Sixty-One (seat61.com)

Transform Scotland (transformscotland.org.uk)

Transport Scotland (transport.gov.scot)

West Highland Community Rail Partnership (westhighlandcrp.com)

YouTube selection 2019:
   A Guide to Railways in Scotland (VisitScotland 2018)
      All the Stations (channel, 2017) including Episodes 55 Glasgow–Corrour, 56 Corrour–Fort William Mallaig/Kyle Line, 57 Inverness to Carnoustie, 58 Perth to Inverness, 59 Inverness to Wick
   Aberdeen to Inverness driver's eye view (video125co 2011)
   Britain's 10 Most Scenic Rail Journeys (TrainsTrainsTrains 2018)
   Caledonian Sleeper (British Trains Hub 2018)
   Driver's Eye View: Highland Line (British Trains Hub 2018)
   Great Scenic Rail Journeys of Scotland (Airborne Lens 2016)
   Rail Away: Schotland (Inverness–Kyle) (Rail Away TV) (Dutch commentary)
   Railroad Journeys Around the World – Scotland 8169 (Questar 2016)
   Scotland Shorts – great rail journeys (VisitScotland 2017)
   Scotland's Railway – Better in the Making (Network Rail 2019)
   Steam in the Highlands – The Jacobite (Joseph Fusco 2017)
   The West Highland Line – Road to the Isles (northernvibe 2012)
   Train Trip Summary…..Glasgow to Fort William (Yasunari Ishii 2019)

Index

RELATED TITLES FROM CROWOOD

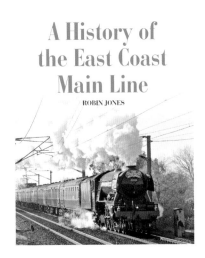

A History of the East Coast Main Line
ROBIN JONES

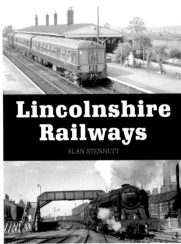

Lincolnshire Railways
ALAN STENNETT

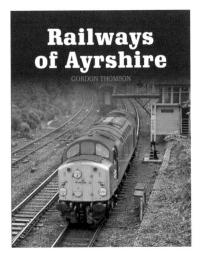

Railways of Ayrshire
GORDON THOMSON

RAILWAYS THROUGH THE VALE OF THE WHITE HORSE
Adrian Vaughan

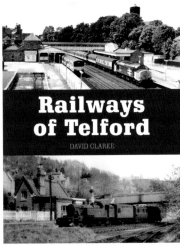

Railways of Telford
DAVID CLARKE

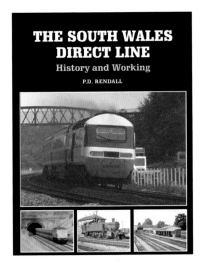

THE SOUTH WALES DIRECT LINE
History and Working
P.D. RENDALL